(continued from previous page)

"Your books have saved my GPA, and quite possibly my sanity. My course grade is now an 'A', and I couldn't be happier."

Student, Winchester, IN

"These books are the best review books on the market. They are fantastic!"

Student, New Orleans, LA

"Your book was responsible for my success on the exam. . . I will look for REA the next time I need help."

Student, Chesterfield, MO

"I think it is the greatest study guide I have ever used!"

Student, Anchorage, AK

"I encourage others to buy REA because of their superiority. Please continue to produce the best quality books on the market."

Student, San Jose, CA

"Just a short note to say thanks for the great support your book gave me in helping me pass the test . . . I'm on my way to a B.S. degree because of you !"

Student, Orlando, FL

Super Review®

All You Need to Know!

GENETICS

By the Staff of
Research & Education Association
Dr. M. Fogiel, Chief Editor

Research & Education Association
61 Ethel Road West
Piscataway, New Jersey 08854

SUPER REVIEW®
OF GENETICS

Printed in the United States of America

Library of Congress Control Number 2003098210

International Standard Book Number 0-7386-0018-0

SUPER REVIEW® and REA® are registered trademarks of
Research & Education Association, Piscataway, New Jersey 08854.

WHAT THIS **Super Review** WILL DO FOR YOU

This **Super Review** provides all that you need to know to do your homework effectively and succeed on exams and quizzes.

The book focuses on the core aspects of the subject, and helps you to grasp the important elements quickly and easily.

Outstanding **Super Review** features:

- Topics are covered in logical sequence

- Topics are reviewed in a concise and comprehensive manner

- The material is presented in student-friendly language that makes it easy to follow and understand

- Individual topics can be easily located

- Provides excellent preparation for midterms, finals and in-between quizzes

- In every chapter, reviews of individual topics are accompanied by Questions **Q** and Answers **A** that show how to work out specific problems

- Written by professionals and test experts who function as your very own tutors

Dr. Max Fogiel
Program Director

CONTENTS

Genetics–Simplified Summary *(continued)*

Genetics–Simplified Summary *(continued)*

Genetics Reviews

ix

Genetics–Simplified Summary

The Blueprint for Life

Searching for Secrets

Human ingenuity, science, and technology have combined to discover the mechanisms by which life works. They have produced techniques through which diseases can be treated or prevented. These techniques also give scientists the power to alter and redesign living organisms, giving rise to legal and ethical questions on how this power should be used. In searching for the secret of life we need to begin by obtaining answers to the following questions:

(1) What is the difference between living and non–living things?

(2) How does life exist in all its varieties in many different kinds of environmental conditions?

(3) How are the instructions, vital for making an organism, passed on from one generation to the next?

The answer to all of the preceding questions may be found in DNA.

DNA, which stands for deoxyribonucleic acid, is a long, thin, thread–like material. The length of DNA found in one human being is 200 times greater than the distance from the earth to the sun. DNA is a remarkable molecule. It contains the blueprint for life.

James Watson and Francis Crick, in the early 1950's, discovered how DNA is able to do this. DNA has the shape of a double helix and is composed of a carbohydrate backbone. Inside the grooves of the double helix, extending from the carbohydrate backbone, are molecules called nucleotides or bases that are designated by the initials A, G, T, or C.

All information and instructions for life contained in DNA are written in a code consisting of these four molecules. A single instruction is encoded by a piece of DNA called a gene, some of which may be thousands of letters long. The instructions needed to specify

The Watson & Crick model of DNA, the blueprint for life.

an entire human being are six billion code letters long. Every cell, in its nucleus, contains all the information needed to produce a human being. This information is contained in many long strands of DNA, which themselves are separated into chromosomes. The DNA of a human is found in 23 pairs of chromosomes. Every organism that is living, or has lived, contains DNA which spells out that organism's specific instructions for life.

Life at the Beginning

Charles Darwin believed that life originated in a warm pond. Today, however, biologist Karl Stetter believes that life originated in an environment similar to that of the sulfurous ponds in Sulfatar Crater near Naples, Italy, where the temperature is very hot (96°C) and there is little oxygen available. Stetter believes it was under these conditions that the proper ingredients came together to make life possible.

DNA was not present in the early earth environment, but Stetter believes when organisms were first formed they had DNA. Stetter studies the conditions of primitive earth by simulating them in giant fermentation vessels in his laboratory in Regensburg, Germany. Until recently, many scientists did not believe that life could exist

Early life is thought to have originated in an environment similar to the Sulfatar Crater in Italy.

in such an environment; however, Stetter has discovered many species of bacteria that can live in these conditions. Not only can these bacteria live at very high temperatures, they can utilize sulfur for energy and do so in the absence of oxygen.

These species of bacteria are thought to be living descendants of an ancestral form of life. Contained within these bacteria are the DNA instructions for surviving in such a primitive earth–like environment, the same DNA instructions used by the ancestral form of life to survive in similar conditions.

Because of its unique double helical structure, DNA has the ability to pass on its instructions to the next generation. The DNA double helix can unwind and each strand be used as a model to copy the instructions. In this way DNA can pass its information from generation to generation. While extinction of an organism will obviously stop this process, this does not mean the DNA from these organisms cannot be studied.

Amber, a material found in pine resin, can preserve small organisms such as insects. Some of these preserved samples may be as much as 25 to 100 million years old. These ancient insects are used by entomologists to make comparisons between ancient and modern insects. Entomologists theorized that if tissue survived in these preserved specimens intact, DNA could be isolated.

Ancient DNA

The DNA instructions from these ancient specimens could contribute to the knowledge of insect evolution. The preserved DNA can be extracted, amplified, and analyzed using laboratory techniques. The order of the four bases which make up the DNA is then determined by sequencing the DNA. By using these methods, scientists can determine the instructions encoded in the DNA of extinct insects. By examining the genetic code of these and other organisms, scientists can gain insight into how extinct organisms lived and evolved into their modern forms. DNA contains the instructions for making an organism, therefore, by studying the DNA, scientists are studying the organism.

It is possible that if the entire DNA sequence was known for an organism, that organism could be wholly reconstructed. This is the premise used for the movie *Jurassic Park* and realized to a smaller extent in the laboratory. For instance, a blood-sucking insect, which has been extinct for 70 to 80 million years, may contain blood cells from its most recent meal, perhaps a dinosaur. These dinosaur cells could contain intact DNA which could be analyzed and sequenced. However, in order to recreate a dinosaur, all of the DNA must be preserved intact. This possibility is minuscule.

DNA—Our Personal Blueprint

All the DNA found in human cells is referred to as the human genome. The human genome has been sequenced and decoded in laboratories around the world as part of ongoing multibillion dollar projects to read the entire six billion letter codes of human DNA. DNA is made up of genes which are individual sets of instructions encoding for such diverse features as hair color to the structure of enzymes found in the digestive system. Genes encode all the information required to put together the parts making up an organism.

Decoding the human genome will lead to new ways to prevent, treat, and cure disease. At the National Institutes of Health in Bethesda, Maryland, Craig Venter and his team of scientists are studying the genes that comprise the DNA of the human brain.

Dr. Venter believes that the genes in the brain may be important in the specific functions of the brain. This represents approximately one–third of the entire human genome. These genes are involved in personality, brain processes, and general brain function. Humans are defined by these processes. Scientists believe that by studying these genes they are finding the answers to questions about human life. The brain is at the center of that which makes us human, so studying the brain may lead to a better understanding of ourselves.

In order to find and analyze these genes, DNA is extracted from frozen human brain tissue and cleaved into fragments. Venter's team of scientists, however, only studies the genes that are vital in brain operation. These brain–specific DNA fragments can be amplified into millions of copies by placing the DNA of interest into a specific microbe and growing it in the laboratory. The process is repetitive and time–consuming.

The next step, which is mostly automated, is to sequence the DNA and find out the order of the billions of chemical codes. Assisted by computers, the fragments of DNA sequence are strung together to form longer and longer strands of DNA. Scientists are then able to analyze the DNA sequences and the genes.

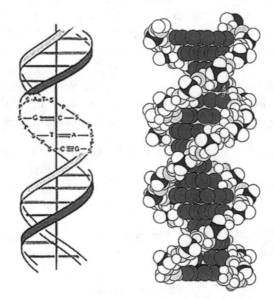

A DNA chain contains the genetic codes for life.

From Flies to Elephants

Shared Secrets

Every form of life shares the same chemical structure of DNA, from bacteria to man. By looking at the sequence of DNA it is possible to tell what organism the DNA came from. In addition, many genes are shared between organisms. Humans share the same genetic information with many other organisms. For instance, parts of the DNA that makes up the human brain also makes up the brains of flies or elephants. Dr. Venter observes that by studying organisms at this level, scientists find that all the species on earth are related. Therefore, by studying the DNA of other organisms, scientists may be able to learn something about humans.

Because of this relatedness, other organisms' genomes are also being sequenced and analyzed. In Cambridge, England, another of the Human Genome Project scientists, John Sulston, studies the genome of the nematode. The nematode is a worm, a millimeter in length, which lives in forest soil. The nematode's life span is very short. The features and mechanisms of the nematode, once discerned, can also be found in humans. The adult nematode contains 1,000 cells. Sulston studies the growth of the nematode from one cell to the adult form. More is known about the nematode than any other creature. This detail has made the nematode a popular organism for scientists to deduce the mechanisms of living things.

Many scientists believe that understanding how genes work in a simple organism is less complicated than studying the same mechanisms in an organism which is comprised of millions or billions of cells. An embryo is a single egg cell which has just been fertilized. It receives half of its DNA from its mother and half from its father.

As the embryo develops, its cells divide. The one cell embryo undergoes the first division and becomes two new cells, each with its own nucleus. Each time a cell divides to become two daughter cells, the DNA must replicate and distribute itself evenly between the two cells. This process can be recorded and then viewed by scientists. As the embryo grows it elongates; as muscles develop they begin to twitch. It all begins as one cell but develops into an organism with a total of 1,000 cells. The production of tissue developing in the embryo (muscles, neurons, skin, intestines, etc.) is controlled by genes. These genes also control behavior.

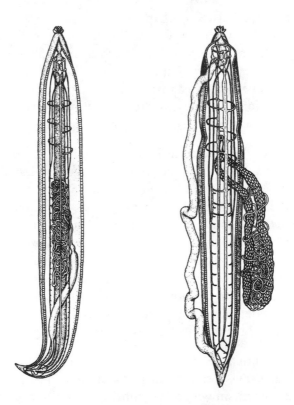

Nematode genomes are being sequenced and analyzed to determine how their DNA works.

Mutations

A mutant is an organism that is defective in a particular gene. There is a mutant nematode that does not transmit signals from nerves to muscle. These mutants are called "*unc*" mutants because they are *unc*oordinated. This mutant does not move as elegantly as the normal worm, whose scientific name is *C. nioditid elegans*, instead it either shudders or cannot move at all. Dr. Sulston believes that the mutation is in the transmission of the signal from the nervous system to the muscle. In order to discover the gene responsible for this defect and others of interest, the entire genome of the nematode is being sequenced. Dr. Sulston believes that the method by which the genomes are elucidated are the same whether it is the human or the nematode project. The point is to discover as much information as possible. The nematode has about 1% the amount of human DNA, but because worms and humans are related, the sequence of the worm's DNA is similar to human DNA. Sulston believes that with the study of a few organisms: bacteria, yeast, nematode, fly, and humans, scientists can discover all the mechanisms of life. This is the basis of the Human Genome Project.

Genes Controlling Development

A human embryo also grows from a single cell to a multicellular organism: a baby, which contains millions of cells. The genes that control this complex process of growth and development are being elucidated in several organisms including humans but also in the nematode, fruit flies, and chicks. The genes involved in other processes are also being searched for. The gene that determines sex in humans has been discovered. The genes that cause aging and death are being investigated and the search for the breast cancer gene may soon prove successful.

DNA is being moved from one animal to another, and genetic engineering has allowed scientists to create farm animals containing human genes. Animals producing human drugs in milk and blood are very valuable. In addition, human embryos can be diagnosed with certain genetic diseases by studying the DNA from a single cell of an unborn child.

Human beings with genetic diseases from cancer to AIDS are being treated by replacement of their defective gene with a non–defective gene. Also, this genetic information is changing social perceptions of the very definition of human beings and their creation. For example, there is only a 1% difference between the DNA of a human and a chimp. The relatedness of species goes far beyond this comparison.

Our Cousin, the Yeast?

Another example is found in Oxford, England at Oxford University. Here Paul Nurse holds the theory that all life is elaborations on the same theme. Nurse concludes that as nature changes the demands it makes on organisms, additional components are added to compensate. Thus, organisms are always evolving to the demands of nature. This theory holds that all organisms are related on the DNA level. To test his concept, Nurse devised an experiment to test if a single–celled yeast could read and understand the information coded for by human DNA.

Mechanisms of the Yeast Cell

Yeast are organisms consisting of only one cell and it is they who are responsible for making bread rise and beer alcoholic. Dr. Nurse compares the mechanisms of cells with that of a motorcycle. The motorcycle is made up of many different parts that alone would not work as a motorcycle. The cell is made up of many different parts, which taken together, form a functioning cell. Studying the parts or mechanisms is what is of interest to scientists such as Nurse.

Specifically, Nurse is interested in the mechanism by which cells divide. His method is to study cells that do not function properly. Scientists can make mutations in genes and then study how the organism works with the mutant gene. This method can tell the scientist which mechanism the gene is involved in. To study cell division, Nurse grows yeast on laboratory plates. Yeast cells grow to a certain size, at which time they divide into two new cells. Mutants in this process cannot divide and do not grow well as a result. Yeast cells that contain the mutant gene *cdc2* cannot divide but can continue to grow. Nurse wants to find the human homologue to the yeast *cdc2* gene.

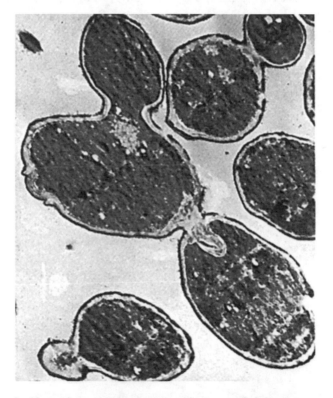

In Nurse's experiment, mutant yeast cells were given pieces of human DNA to determine if the yeast cells would incorporate the human gene.

Nurse's strategy was to give the mutant yeast cells pieces of human DNA. If a mutant yeast cell uptakes the human *cdc2* gene and can read and understand the instructions, then that mutant can be cured or repaired. The repaired yeast will grow and divide normally. The DNA that Nurse used was from a DNA library of human genes. The human gene must perform the same function as the yeast gene in order for the experiment to work and for the yeast cells to grow and divide normally.

Humans and yeast shared an ancestor a billion years ago. Since then they have evolved separately. For Nurse's experiment to work, the yeast must recognize the DNA from a human. Nurse was able to show that human DNA did contain a homologue for the yeast *cdc2* gene and that mutant yeast were able to recognize and carry out the instructions of human DNA. The mutant yeast, after incubation with the human gene, were able to grow and divide normally. It might be said that the mutant yeast were cured.

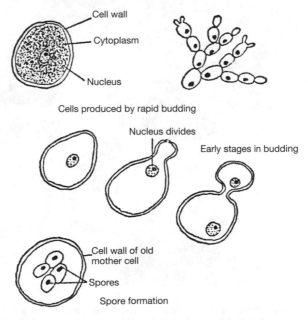

Cell wall

Cytoplasm

Nucleus

Cells produced by rapid budding

Nucleus divides

Early stages in budding

Cell wall of old mother cell

Spores

Spore formation

Budding yeast cells show how Nurse's yeast cells would grow and divide normally.

Conservation of Cellular Mechanisms

Once nature has evolved a good mechanism for doing something it becomes universal and is said to be conserved between species. Nurse believes the *cdc2* gene is an ancient gene that has been conserved because its function is essential to all living organisms. Nurse believes that humans have added on many other mechanisms resulting in a large part of the human genome. Humans possess the genes which encode for all the physical functions and characteristics of noses and heads, yeast obviously do not. Nurse concludes that the part of the human genome which is shared with yeast is ancient and has been conserved over time.

The data derived from the Human Genome Project will be useful in understanding life's mechanisms not only in man, but also in such organisms as yeast and nematodes. Dr. Nurse believes the knowledge that humans share genes with worms and yeast should give humans a greater respect for living organisms.

The Universal Code

All organisms share a common gene pool because all organisms evolved from a common ancestor. That common ancestor was created in the primordial conditions of early Earth along with DNA. Scientists are searching for a direct descendant of the first living organisms. Investigators such as Karl Stetter continue to sample volcanic–like environments in search of organisms. The bacteria from these volcanic hot spots are collected and their DNA is analyzed.

Stetter believes the bacteria found in this environment are the direct descendants of the first living organism and, as a result, the DNA should be similar. After collecting his samples, Stetter takes them to his laboratory and freezes them in liquid nitrogen for storage. After thawing, the organisms are still alive and can grow normally. As might be expected, these organisms are very hardy creatures and can survive the hot conditions in volcanoes and the freezing temperatures of liquid nitrogen. When a comparison is made, Stetter finds these organisms are not only similar to bacteria but also to other higher organisms including man. Stetter believes these organisms to be man's primitive ancestors.

The DNA of these primitive ancestors has been inherited by all living organisms including humans. It has been replicated numerous times over 3.5 billion years and has evolved into equally numerous variations. Human DNA, then, contains not only the information to make a human, but also genes that are shared with other

Chimpanzees are man's closest evolutionary relative. Many chimpanzees display some human-like attributes.

organisms. DNA can be perceived not only as an archive of human genetic history, but also of the future, since it continues to be passed on to future generations.

Man and Ape: Neighbors on the Evolutionary Tree

As life evolved from the primordial soup, species developed that were better able to adapt and thrive in the conditions found on ancient Earth. These changes, occurring over billions of years, have given us the incredible variety of plants and animals we see today. Scientists believe that man's closest evolutionary relative is the ape. Around six million years ago there was a change in our common ancestor that resulted in a "split" in the evolutionary tree and allowed for the separate development of man and ape.

The search for our past has led researchers to eastern Africa in the area of the present-day countries of Ethiopia and Kenya. In particular, the region around the Awash River in northern Ethiopia has

Paleontologists believe that modern man evolved from ape-like ancestors.

proven to be extremely fertile ground for paleontologists searching for evidence of our ancient ancestors. In 1974, the fossil of a three million-year-old female was discovered. Given the scientific name *Australopithecus afarensis* and the nickname Lucy, she was, at that time, the oldest known member of the human family and thought to have belonged to the first species that evolved after the human/ape evolutionary split. Almost 20 years later, two additional fossil discoveries were made, both in the Awash River region of Ethiopia. One fossil discovered was of a male believed to be a descendant of Lucy. The other fossil predated Lucy by around 1.5 million years, placing it even closer to the common ancestor of man and ape.

After studying the fossils, scientists postulated that the *Australopithecus afarensis* were quite an adaptable group. This ability to adapt allowed them to survive in their changing environment. It is thought that they ate fruit, bugs and small animals, had no tools except maybe sticks for digging, and had learned to walk before they developed complex thought. The males of the species stood approximately five feet tall and weighed only 100 pounds. Females were believed to be about a foot shorter and 25 pounds

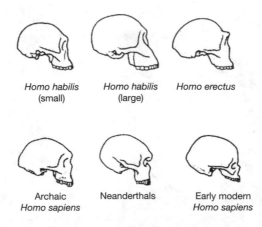

Homo habilis   Homo habilis   Homo erectus
(small)   (large)

Archaic   Neanderthals   Early modern
Homo sapiens   Homo sapiens

Early man had an ape-like face and protruding jaw. Through the process of evolution, early man's skull changed to resemble modern man.

lighter. They had apelike faces with prominent foreheads and protruding jaws. Their brains were no bigger than a chimp's. Over time, as their brains evolved, *Australopithecus* underwent an evolutionary split to form a second species. Over the next two to three million years, that new species evolved to eventually produce *Homo sapiens*, modern man.

A paleontologist shows a fossil fragment of *Australopithecus afarensis*, a specimen of early man.

Evolution and DNA

By analyzing DNA from different organisms scientists have found that DNA is universal among living things. It has taken science to prove a connection which aboriginal and native peoples have all along believed to be true – that all living things are related. Throughout history, humans have separated themselves because of their differences. The ability to analyze DNA has made it clear that there are many more similarities than differences. All living things share an evolutionary history. DNA is the unifying factor in all living things, yet it is variations which exist in DNA that are responsible for the diversity of life.

Life: Master Plan or Accident?

Survival

Chimpanzees and humans share many similar traits and genetic material

Does nature use a plan to design life as we know it, or is life, including humans, "an accident of creation?" Human beings and chimpanzees are similar in some ways but also very different from each other. Differences between humans and chimpanzees are due to an accumulation of "mistakes" in the DNA. Little mistakes are made in each generation. After many generations, there are enough mistakes to create two different species from one.

One of the most important aspects of the secret of life is its ability to change. The mistakes made over time permit life to adapt and evolve. This theory of evolution was originated by Charles Darwin. People of Darwin's time were interested in the great diversity of nature. It was this interest that lead to the theory that life changes over time and, over long periods of time, these changes result in new species.

An example of the diversity of life can be found in the African butterfly. African butterflies from the same species have numerous differences in the pattern on their wings. Darwin believed that new species could emerge as a result of these little differences. Darwin thought life began as simple organisms that accumulated differences over time.

Eventually, new species emerged from that simple form of life. After billions of generations, hundreds of millions of species, including the 30 million species which currently inhabit the earth, could have emerged. Darwin did not know how these changes occurred from generation to generation. DNA was the answer to Darwin's problem of how differences can occur and how they are inherited.

DNA contains the instructions for making organisms. Each time a cell divides, its DNA is duplicated such that the next generation

Charles Darwin originated the theory of evolution in nature.

of cells contains the same instructions as the past generation. It is in the duplication of DNA that differences can occur and where the mechanism of evolution is found. Because of its length, there are mistakes made when copying the billions of bases making up the DNA code. Under normal circumstances the cell detects these mistakes and corrects them, but occasionally some of these are missed. These mistakes in copying the DNA can result in mutations. The mechanism of evolution is the introduction of mutations into DNA.

Cultural Concepts of Mutation

Culturally, mutations have been portrayed as causing freaks of nature or creating monsters. For instance, in a film called *Them* made in the 1950's, the DNA of ants was mutated by the radiation of an atomic bomb. The ants were portrayed as killers which had to be destroyed in order for humans to survive. But in fact, without mutations the human race would not be here at all. Without mutations, life could not continue.

Mutation and Evolution

The island chain of Hawaii can be used as an example of how mutations can influence the evolution of life. The Hawaiian Islands are representative of evolution in action. Six million years ago the Hawaiian Islands began as volcanic rock in the middle of the Pacific Ocean. The island chain was isolated from all other land masses. The islands were as earth once was, a lifeless rock. Living organisms soon migrated from other places. Insects arrived at the islands by wind or by sea on floating logs. Birds flew to the islands and brought seeds. New species arrived by accident from other lands and found their new environment different from their points of origination. These original species adapted to life in a new environment and over time have evolved into the variety of plant and animal species now native to the Hawaiian Islands. Hawaii is now filled with life. The early organisms that accidentally reached the islands had to learn to live in the new environment, to adapt. Mutations allowed the species to adapt to these changes in living conditions and are the reason why these organisms were so successful.

The Developing Organism

Order from Disorder

The formation of all animals begins with a single cell, the fertilized egg. After numerous divisions, a multicellular organism is ultimately created, made up of billions of cells. As the fertilized egg begins to divide, the progeny cells formed look alike and seem to move without direction; however, as divisions continue and time passes, patterns begin to form and structure and order are achieved. Masses of cells move in concert, folding and sliding together.

In humans, two weeks from the initial division of the fertilized egg, the spinal cord starts to take form. Cells move together in a line and begin to take the shape of a tube. Muscles begin to form in blocks alongside the developing spinal cord. The primitive heart has begun to beat. The initial, seemingly chaotic, random movements and divisions are beginning to have meaning and purpose. The making of an organism takes on direction: on one end, there will be the tail; on the other end, a head. Certain cells take on specific functions that are different from other cells. For instance, cells in the heart function to pump blood, whereas cells in the eye function to provide vision. Cells somehow know their orientation in the body plan and what their function will be. For example, the cells in the developing chick surround the embryo and use the yolk as a nutritional source for the growing organism.

Basic Body Plans

Basic body plans are already established in the two–day–old chick embryo. These plans establish where the limbs will grow and that there will be feathers, among other things. Humans are both similar and very different. The difference is not in the cells, but in the arrangement of the cells in development. The different arrangement of cells will determine if this organism will have hair on its skin, like human beings, or feathers, like chicks. Similar arrangement of cells will determine that humans and chicks will both have bones, skin, blood, livers, hearts and brains. There are no brain cells found in a toe, or eye cells in an elbow. The heart always forms in the same place at the same time. How cells know where and what to differentiate into is the focus of many studies.

Ultrasound can give parents a glimpse of their developing baby, but it is not a complete view. A pregnant woman can see her baby's head as well as details of it: the face and the ears, for example. The doctor can tell expectant mothers the sex of their child and can see the formation of fingers and toes. The local environment of cells provides them with signals to tell them what type of cells to differ-

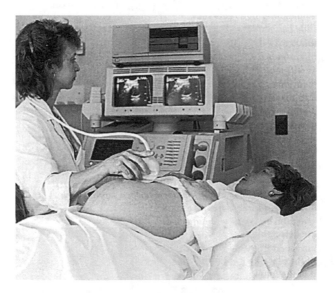

An ultrasound can be used to detect some genetic problems with an unborn child.

entiate into. Mistakes are made when cells cannot understand the local environmental signals. For example, if cells cannot tell the difference between left and right, development is affected.

In one neonatal condition, an infant can be born with functioning organ systems which are perfectly normal but are located on the opposite sides of the body. In normal individuals, the heart and stomach are on the left side of the body and the liver is on the right side, but in mirror image organ systems, the heart and stomach are on the right and the liver is on the left. In this case, ultrasound can be used to detect this problem. Fortunately this condition is not fatal. Babies affected by it can grow to be normal and healthy and should not have any complications in the future.

Harmful Mutations

Sadly, other mistakes in development can be more serious. There is a condition in which the heart, which normally should be on the left side of the body, is located on the right. In addition, the heart itself is not formed properly. The collecting chambers of the heart are not separated and there may be a hole between the left and right pumping chambers.

This heart condition can prevent babies from properly oxygenating their blood. In this condition the developing cells knew right from left except for the cells destined to become the heart. The heart is a complex organ and its development is equally complex. The embryonic heart develops from a forked tube of cells. This heart begins to beat as blood vessels are forming throughout the body. The embryonic heart tube twists to the right as the chambers begin to form. The blood vessels connect to the heart and to each other, the result being a functioning circulatory system.

In humans, this entire series of events occurs before the heart is a quarter of an inch long. In this condition, however, during development, the heart twisted to the left side of the body instead of the right. The blood vessels expected the heart to twist to the right as it normally should have.

When it does not, the connection between the heart and blood vessels are not formed properly. This condition can be corrected by surgery but will result in a weakened heart. The affected child will survive but will not be able to participate in sports and physical activities to the same extent as other children and will also require continued care. In this condition the cells may have read an ancestral message. Scientists theorize there was a primordial organism that was entirely one–sided due to an asymmetry message read by their cells. The descendants of these organisms are more symmetrical (as are humans), but still have within them the ancient message of asymmetry.

The Cell: Where to Go, What to Become?

The ability of cells to tell directions (right and left) is important in the formation of organ systems. It is also critical that cells can differentiate top from bottom, or head from tail. Each of the cells of the developing embryo contain the exact same genetic information, exactly the same instructions for making a complete organism. The question scientists ask themselves is, if each cell contains the same genetic information, how are they able to differentiate into functionally different cells?

Scientists have chosen the fruit fly, *Drosophila melanogaster*, as the organism with which to study this problem. Drosophila were bred to produce mutants whose body plans were not normal. For example, some of these flies have legs in place of antennae on their head.

While most scientists were looking at the adult fly, Professor Christiane Nusslein–Volhard, from her laboratory in Biebenhausen, Germany, was the first to look at the larva of fruit flies and to discover how cells know anterior from posterior. Nusslein–Volhard found that the larval stage was mostly ignored by scientists because larva spend most of their life cycle in the food of the flies. This makes them difficult to study. Through hard work, Nusslein–Volhard found mutant larva with altered body plans.

The first structures visible in the fly's egg are segments which form along its length. The basic body plan pattern is established by these segments on the length of the embryo. Nusslein–Volhard found mutants that alter this segmentation. These mutations can result in individuals who have two posterior ends or just one end. These mutants do not survive.

Nusslein–Volhard found the genes responsible for these muta-tions and isolated them. She also found that cells in the embryo are

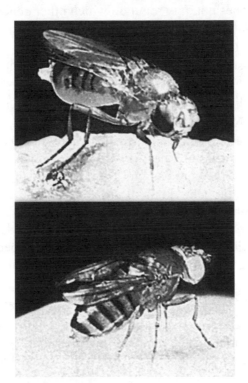

Drosophila **have been bred to inten-tionally produce mutants for study.**

able to tell tail from head by chemical messages from the mother already present in the egg. The chemical messages are different in the head and tail. The front-end chemical messages can turn on a control gene that stimulates the expression of many other genes, all responsible for the production of anterior cells. Tail-end chemical messages activate control genes involved in the production of posterior cells. A cell's fate then is determined by its position in the egg of the fly.

Control Genes

Control genes not only regulate which other genes will be activated, but also the time and place of their activation. The control genes respond to signals already in place in the egg and turn on the specific instructions that tell the cell its fate. Since the discovery of these control genes in flies, they have also been found in the DNA of other animals.

Professor Nusslein–Volhard and other scientists have begun to study the zebrafish, an organism whose body plan is closer to that of humans. Zebrafish are ideal organisms in which to study development because they are easy to grow, but the study of zebrafish development is far behind that of *Drosophila*. The development of a zebrafish embryo from the single fertilized egg to a multicellular organism made up of millions of cells takes just ten days. Zebrafish have a generation time of two months, that is, they become capable of reproducing at this time. They can produce up to 400 progeny per week and are transparent, as a result, development can be viewed under a microscope.

Zebrafish are being studied to find the chemical signals and control genes that are activated so that the organ systems form in the right place and at the correct time in development.

Zebrafish and human development is not as different as one might expect. Both organisms develop from a single fertilized egg. Almost every cell in the respective organism has the exact same genetic information. A gene which is expressed only in the liver is in the genetic information of every cell of the body. Even though all the cells in the body contain this gene, it only works in the liver. This specific activation is allowed by the control gene.

Cells in the developing embryo can tell when it is time for the liver to develop and, at that time, the genes needed to make the liver are turned on in those cells. Control genes in other organs are also turned on during development. These control genes are switches that turn on an entire cascade of specific genes that will determine what cells make up the lungs, muscle and brain, for example. The mechanisms of these control switches are still being studied.

Death and the Sexes

DNA Determines Your Sex

The control gene that determines the sex of a human being is found on the Y chromosome. Of the 23 pairs of chromosomes, 22 pairs are homologous and 1 pair is not. These are the X and Y chromosomes, or the sex chromosomes. An individual with two X chromosomes is a female. An individual with one X and one Y chromosome is a male.

A person gets half of the genetic information from the father and half from the mother. The person must receive an X chromosome from the mother. The person can get either an X or a Y chromosome from the father. If a person receives an X chromosome from the father, then that person will be female. If a person receives a Y chromosome from the father, then that person will be a male.

Scientists studied what specific characteristics of the Y chromosome make a male. As technology improved, it became clear to scientists that just having the X or Y chromosome did not determine sex. There were individuals who had both an X and a Y chromosome and were female. There were also individuals who had two X chromosomes but were male. The DNA of the XX males revealed that these individuals carried a small part of the Y chromosome in their genomes. The small region contained the *sry* gene which is responsible for maleness. Scientists have used the mouse model to study sex determination.

The *sry* gene was added to the genes of a developing female mouse embryo. This experiment was used to test whether it was this gene that made an individual a male. This embryo grew to be a male mouse. This experiment proved that the *sry* gene could make an XX female into a male. If nobody had this *sry* gene then everybody would be female. Sex determination is a marvelous mechanism. In a period of days, in a few thousand cells, one gene can influence the development of a male or a female. Individuals who have both an X and a Y chromosome, but are missing the *sry* gene, will develop as females.

Individuals can also have the X and Y chromosomes and the *sry* gene and be female. In this case, the cells were not able to understand the male switch. During development the *sry* gene was present and was switched on, and testes started to develop. However, the body could not recognize testosterone as a signal for maleness and testicular development was not completed. Not being able to understand the male testosterone signal is also a genetic condition.

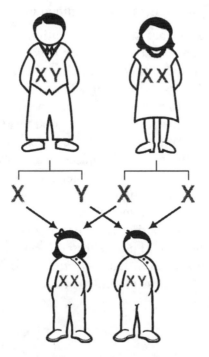

DNA determines the sex of human beings.

Some disorders can be corrected if they are caught early in development. For example, there is a condition in which a baby can be born with two X chromosomes and ovaries, but with male genitalia due to the production of testosterone by a faulty adrenal gland. This condition can be corrected surgically and with hormone treatments. After treatment, the baby will anatomically grow to be a normal healthy female and will also be able to have children. These cases illustrate the difficulty in defining sex by the chromosomes an individual possesses.

Since the 1960's, sex tests have been used in athletics to prevent males from competing as females. Sex tests before 1968 consisted of visual inspection of external genitalia. However, at the Mexico City Olympics a new test was employed, the Barr Body test. The Barr Body test is used to determine the presence of a second X chromosome. A few cells from the wall of the cheek can be used. These cells are stained and examined microscopically.

Despite evidence that sex determination was based on other factors aside from chromosomes, the test was used until 1992. Some women's athletic careers may have been ruined by this test. Starting at the 1992 Winter Olympics in Albertville, France, a new test was used to test for the presence of the *sry* gene. However, most scientists still do not believe there is a good test to determine sex. Many believe what is really being tested is testosterone levels. Testosterone can cause an increase in muscle mass. However, testosterone levels are independent of the *sry* gene. Consider the following: an XY female can have a mutation in the *sry* gene that renders the *sry* gene product nonfunctional. These individuals are women but are excluded from competing in athletic events. Some scientists believe that athletes should not be tested for their genetic sex. It is difficult to define sex tests that truly tell the difference between men and women. The test currently in use can be unfair to some women.

Death and DNA

Control genes are powerful in sex determination and their effects are lifelong. Their effects last from conception through childhood, puberty, and into adulthood. Scientists have wondered if there are also controls on aging and death. Are these events preprogrammed in our genes? Over the past 100 years, the average life span of an individual has increased to about 75 years. In the same way that there are control genes that begin development, there may be genes that control aging. Cells may be programmed to divide a certain number of times and then die.

Werner's Syndrome is a genetic disease causing premature aging in individuals. Dr. Sydney Shall studies this disease at Sussex University in England. One possible hypothesis is that people affected by the disease have their aging clocks set faster than normal; this causes them to age faster. Dr. Shall has found that the mutation responsible for Werner's Syndrome affects the rate at which tissue can regenerate. Tissue is constantly regenerating in the body, in wound healing, for example.

Aging may be defined in two ways: by decay and damage to the brain and damage to the tissues of the rest of the body. Brain tissue is not able to regenerate itself, therefore the damage is permanent. The rest of the body's tissue can regenerate and replace damaged tissue.

Individuals affected by Werner's Syndrome cannot regenerate tissue fast enough. This explains why Werner's Syndrome patients do not have degeneration of brain tissue. Werner's Syndrome does not affect the brain; therefore, the Werner's gene is probably not the aging gene. But there is also evidence that aging is not predetermined by our genes at all. Dr. James Vaupel is trying to find out if there is a genetic time clock on life span. He knew people were living longer, but was there a limit on how old people can get? To find his answer, Dr. Vaupel went to Scandinavia to study mortality records. After studying the detailed Swedish records of older individuals from 1750 to 1950, Vaupel believed the upper limit to aging, if there is any, is well beyond 100 years of age. More and more people are living to see their 100th birthday.

Living Longer

Vaupel found that prior to World War II, there were very few people living beyond 100 years of age. Since World War II, however, there have been more and more people living to 100 years and beyond. Vaupel estimates there are currently 30,000 people in the world above the age of 100 and this number doubles every seven to eight years. Dr. Vaupel also studied a unique archive of twin studies maintained since 1870 in Denmark. Examination of these files revealed that of the 50,000 identical twins, who, by definition, have exactly the same genes, most do not die at the same age, as one might expect if death is genetically predetermined. Vaupel does not believe there is a genetic clock with a predetermined time of death. The evidence appears to confirm there is not a genetic determination to aging and death. Many people view aging as another step of development, however, Vaupel does not believe his studies necessarily support that statement. Vaupel believes that children born today have a good chance of seeing their 100th birthdays. He also predicts a large increase in the elderly population during the next century.

There are 3.3 million people over the age of 85 in the United States. By the year 2080, officials predict 18.7 million, and this number could reach 72 million in 2080 if there is not a genetically predetermined age of death, as Dr. Vaupel believes. A population explosion of this sort could have serious social consequences.

The evidence so far indicates there are no death genes in our genetic instructions. Then how and why do organisms die? One intriguing example is the Pacific salmon, where one species may live for five years, while another has an average life span of only two years. Salmon hatch in mountain streams and immediately swim toward the ocean. In the ocean, the fish mature to adulthood. After years in the ocean, the salmon make their way back to the same spawning ground where they were hatched. Salmon then die after laying their eggs.

A Secondary Issue?

Reproduction, not death, is the important issue in biology. Once an individual has successfully reproduced it has guaranteed the continuation of the species. What happens to the individual following reproduction is, in evolutionary terms, irrelevant. Dr. James Kirkwood, a zoo veterinarian, studies aging and death in animals. Most animals in the wild are killed by predation, but in zoos they are protected from this hazard.

One of Kirkwood's animals is a 14-year-old South American marmoset. In evolutionary and genetic terms this animal has been a success: it has reproduced and passed on its genes to the next gen-

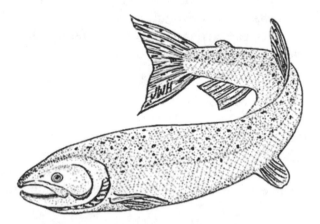

Salmon are genetically driven to reproduce before death.

eration successfully. However, it is still living on. The animal is beginning to show signs of aging. Dr. Kirkwood expects this animal to eventually die of a degenerative disease, such as a tumor. The problems of old age are not the result of genes that cause aging, rather they are caused by the harmful genes that negatively affect post–production–age individuals. Harmful genes that affect individuals before reproduction have, to a great extent, been eliminated by evolution. These genes must be mostly eliminated in order for a species to survive. However, there is no selection against the harmful genes that affect us after reproduction. The products of these genes accumulate and result in symptoms of aging and eventually death. Examples are the genes causing heart disease and cancer. They are responsible for the majority of deaths in older individuals.

Mortality usually strikes individuals when their parents die. Whatever evolution's intentions, aging senior citizens are a cultural resource of wisdom and experience. It is through language, not genes, that this information is passed on through the generations. It is inevitable that our parents, as well as ourselves, will eventually succumb to the processes of aging and death. However, through the mechanisms of evolution, our parents' genes, as well as our own, will be passed on to the next generation. Our ability to communicate and pass on knowledge and experience further increases this genetic immortality.

Genes affect our lives, from conception through death. Genes are immortal because they are passed from one generation to the next. In effect, our parents live on in us because we have their genes and we will live on because we have given our children our genes. The study of our genes may or may not allow us to extend our life spans, but in an evolutionary sense we are already immortal.

Organisms By Design

Genetic Chimeras

Genetic engineers have the capability to change the natural order of things. For instance, genetic engineers can alter the genetic makeup of a tomato. But what exactly have they done to alter the tomato, and is the tomato still a tomato? Biotechnology may give scientists the power to revolutionize medicine and investors the opportunity to profit from this success. The benefits seem clear, but some people caution that this new technology may also bring new concerns.

Nature has always had a particular order to it. What type of organism an embryo will divide and grow into is determined by the genes it carries. Mice pass on mouse genes to their offspring and humans pass on the genes that make them uniquely human. But current scientific techniques and knowledge have given researchers the tools to transfer genes from one organism to another. The genes of a human can be put into pigs, the genes of fish into tomatoes, or elephant genes into mice. The era of organisms by design has begun.

Some of the sheep currently grazing on the hills of Scotland do not, as one might expect, belong to farmers, but are owned by a biotechnology company. They regard these sheep in two ways. First they see a profit for investors who have provided the funds for the research that has led to the creation of these sheep.

Second, this is a good scientific idea put into practice successfully. The ability of scientists to manipulate nature in this way raises many ethical questions. Some people believe that scientists are overstepping their bounds when manipulating nature in this way. They argue that since everything is not known about the natural order of life, life should not be altered by humans.

These sheep peacefully grazing in Scotland look and act the same as normal sheep. However these sheep can be worth $10,000 or more. What makes them so valuable to scientists and investors, and so ethically questionable to their critics, is the presence of a human gene in their normal genetic make–up.

Mythology Becomes Reality

Chimeras are creatures that are part human and part animal. Historically, humans have always been fascinated by this type of creature. For example, the centaur, a figure in Greek mythology, is part horse and part man. This idea of a combination of human and animal is still with us in modern mythology: Dracula, the combination of man and bat, or the werewolf, a combination of man and wolf.

Although the examples given are fictional, genetic chimeras do exist. Since the discovery that DNA is the genetic material, scientists have learned a lot about how the instructions for making an organism work. Genes from any species can now be isolated and

Some sheep are being genetically altered by scientists and researchers.

transplanted into any other species. This scientific fact has now been transformed into an industry built on the power of this new technology.

Children in the eighth grade are learning the techniques of biotechnology. The tools of science are easily manipulated. Experiments can be conducted by these students because of the recent discoveries made in the field. The students can even learn to transfer a gene from one organism into another. Bacteria are used in biotechnology to carry foreign genes. The bacteria used is a common bacteria, *Escherichia coli*, which is normally found in the digestive systems of humans, but is grown in the laboratory in special containers.

A chimera is a creature which is part human, part animal. The creature above is a sheep / goat hybrid.

The bacteria are harvested by scooping them up with a wire and transferring them to a test tube. DNA is added to this test tube containing the bacteria. This mixture is cooled, heated and then cooled again. This is the procedure for transferring genes. The DNA used could be from any species and does not have to be bacterial in origin. The bacteria grow for a day, after which time the foreign DNA has been incorporated by some of the bacteria. Bacteria are able to recognize the foreign gene and carry out its instructions. In order for the bacteria to do this, the usual DNA to RNA to protein pathway is followed. The foreign gene is first transcribed into ribonucleic acid, or RNA. The RNA acts as a messenger to bridge the gap between the information encoded for in the DNA and the final

Bacteria is frequently used to introduce foreign genes into an organism.

manifestation of this information, the proteins in the cell. After being transcribed from DNA, the RNA is translated into a protein by the cell. The DNA is left intact by this procedure and reforms its normal double helix structure. If the genes transferred into the bacteria are of human origin, then the bacteria begin to produce human proteins. In this way, human proteins, including those that may be used as drugs, can be produced in large quantities.

Transgenic Animals: "Little Furry Factories?"

October 14, 1981 was a historical first for scientists and investors alike. It was on this day that biotechnology gained the financial backing of investors on Wall Street. Within the first hour of trading, the value of the new biotechnology stock had tripled. Since then, many billions of dollars have been invested in hundreds of new biotechnology companies. Each of these companies offers the opportunity to produce human proteins that may have therapeutic value in certain medical conditions, including heart attacks, strokes, diabetes, and cancer. Although the investment has been great, the results have been very slow in coming. One of the problems is moving from an experimental scale on the laboratory bench to the large factory production line where huge amounts of materials are needed. This process can be time-consuming and costly.

The problem is creating an artificial system to do what organisms do every day, but on a much larger scale. One biotechnology company takes a different approach. Instead of recreating the living factory with plastic and steel, they are using the living animal. Living animals are then used as factories to produce large amounts of human proteins.

Milk is a good source of expressed human proteins. Blood and urine are other sources of expressed human proteins; however, milk can be harvested easily and large quantities can made daily. Casein is the primary protein found in milk. The gene for casein provided the genetic "on" switch for milk–specific expression of foreign genes. The casein gene is expressed only in milk. The gene has specific elements in the DNA found before the start of the gene. It is these elements that will turn on the gene's expression.

Researchers have manipulated the casein gene in the following manner: first, they put the genetic "on" switch, found in front of the casein gene, at the beginning of a human gene. The next step was to put this new gene back in the genetic material of an experimental animal model, for example, a mouse.

The Transfer of Genetic Material

The transfer of the genetically altered material into a new organism begins with the fertilized egg. The DNA must be surgically inserted into the egg. The fertilized egg at this stage of development is so small that the surgery must be done with the use of a microscope. First, the egg is held in place by a suction tool, then the DNA is injected via a needle, finer than a hair, into the single cell. The needle is inserted through the outer membrane of the egg and into the nucleus. Each egg must be injected individually and then checked for the presence of the genetically engineered piece of DNA.

Mice are used as experimental animal models in many areas of genetic research and study.

The eggs are implanted into a surrogate mother and, after the embryos develop, mice are born. These mice are checked for the presence of the engineered gene. Only a few of the hundreds of mice injected contain the gene. In order for the gene to be expressed, it must be taken up by the DNA of the fertilized egg and the gene product produced in the milk. Mice are then checked for the presence of the gene product in their milk. Mice that produced the human gene product in their milk are considered successfully engineered.

Although the amounts of human protein produced by these mice were not large, researchers had proved the idea workable. This was the first step in developing a process. In order to produce a large quantity of material, the mouse is not an ideal organism because of its size. The mice would not produce the quantities of milk needed for mass production. Dairy animals are used by scientists because they produce large amounts of milk.

Some researchers went to Frank Loew of Tufts University Veterinary School. Dr. Loew saw this new technology as an opportunity to revive a sluggish dairy economy. This new technology offered a new use for dairy animals. Goats were chosen because they reproduce twice as fast as cows and produce large quantities of milk.

Karl Ebert, a colleague of Dr. Loew's, works on the expression of a protein that would be used to treat heart attack patients. The process of expressing this gene is the same in principle as that used in the mice. The gene that is transferred into the animal of choice is called the transgene and the animal which incorporates the gene into its own DNA and expresses the gene product is called the transgenic animal.

The Potential for Profit

The human gene being transplanted into goats is used to treat heart attacks and works by dissolving blood clots. This drug is potentially worth millions of dollars. Each dose would cost more than one thousand dollars. The hope is that each transgenic goat would produce millions of dollars worth of protein in its milk. The scientists must test each baby goat born to see if it contains the engineered DNA. But first, the kids must be born. Even animals that could potentially be worth millions of dollars can have a difficult time during the birthing process; therefore, veterinarians make a concerted effort to save every animal. The kids may be very valuable and are taken from their mothers immediately after birth. They are hand-fed so as to minimize any risk of passing disease from mother to baby. The kids are then tested for the presence of the gene. As yet, transgenic goats that express this clot–busting gene have not been produced. Dr. Loew and his team continue to try to produce these transgenic animals, although it is a long and difficult process.

Transgenic Mice

Transgenic mice can be engineered to produce huge quantities of foreign protein. This technology was developed by John Clark in Edinburgh, Scotland. The technology is similar in principle to the techniques used in making transgenic mice and goats in earlier examples; however, Clark made some significant improvements.

After testing several hundred mice to see if they contained the transgene, in June of 1990, Clark found one mouse that not only contained the gene, but was expressing it in huge quantities. This technology has been applied to sheep. A new biotechnology company was founded on the principles of John Clark's mouse. The proteins that the company hopes to commercialize are Factor–9, a protein used to treat hemophilia, and AAT, a protein used in the treatment of a deadly lung disease. Some sheep are producing 30 grams of AAT per liter of milk.

The choice of expressing human proteins in sheep's milk was an excellent one. The sheep have been called "little furry factories." They are capable of making a lot of product; 30 grams of AAT is worth more than one thousand dollars. The sheep are making product and doing so for little money. These transgenic sheep are worth hundreds of thousands of dollars and are zealously protected by the biotechnology company that owns them. The transgenic sheep are mixed in with many other normal sheep. Only the company knows which are the valuable sheep, producing therapeutic protein, and which are producing normal milk.

Microbial Invaders

Us vs. Them

Deadly epidemics have plagued man since the beginning of time. Today scientists are trying to arrest the progress of and cure diseases such as influenza and AIDS, to name just two. The smallpox virus has killed over a hundred million people throughout history. Today the smallpox virus exists in only two facilities on earth: the Center for Disease Control in Atlanta, Georgia and the Russian equivalent in Moscow, Russia; otherwise, smallpox has been obliterated from the earth.

The Center for Disease Control (CDC) is a dangerous place and, as a result, is maintained under strict security. When the last smallpox viruses are destroyed, it will be the first time man has intentionally caused the extinction of another organism. The smallpox story is a great victory for science and medicine. However, there are still other plagues that exists today, for instance, AIDS, which scientists are working to eradicate in the same successful manner as smallpox.

A constant battle is forged within our bodies between ourselves and the many microbes that exist in the world today. If the microbes succeed, they are able to use humans as a source of food and shelter and, in the process, could potentially make their host sick or could even kill the host. The reason that humans survive such attacks is because we have a defense system that can mount a defense specific for the invader.

The immune system is the defense system that protects us from invaders. Over millions of years, the immune system of humans has been evolving weapons to defend against such attacks. The key to the defense system is its ability to quickly recognize the invader. Unfortunately the invaders, through millions of years, have also been evolving. They are constantly trying to evade the body's defense system by finding its weak spots.

Vaccines

Influenza virus is one of the more successful microbes. In the fall of 1918 it killed twice the number of casualties than in the First World War. The world had met an enemy even deadlier than warfare. Influenza virus killed 20 million people worldwide during this period. Influenza is a virus that is transmitted by water, in the air, or condensed on surfaces. The flu virus returns annually in the winter. It infects 50 million people in the United States and kills about

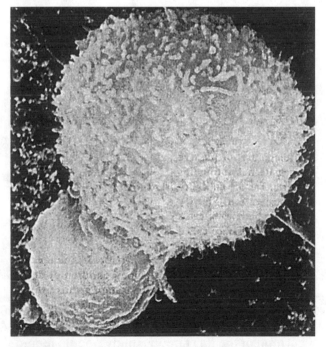

Each year a new influenza virus vaccine must be developed by scientists.

A vaccine for smallpox was developed 200 years ago using the fluid from cowpox, an infection in cows. As this cartoon of the day shows, many people feared the introduction of the foreign material, although it was beneficial.

10,000. Each winter, when the flu virus resurfaces, there is a potential it will unleash another worldwide epidemic.

Vaccines are used to prevent flu. Each year an inactive form of virus is grown in hens' eggs. From these eggs, the flu vaccine is manufactured. New flu vaccines are made each year. Thirty million doses are needed annually. It is the work of the scientists at the CDC in Atlanta to develop a vaccine that will potentially protect the populations of the United States and Europe. Vaccines have been the principle weapons against flu for the past 50 years. The first vaccine was used over 200 years ago by an English country doctor, Edward Jenner, who used the fluid from cowpox, a viral infection in cows, to infect a boy. The cowpox or vaccinia virus results in a mild infection and is protective for the more deadly smallpox. Jenner's ideas were widely ridiculed at the time, but time has shown his theory to be correct.

The Body's Defenses

White blood cells are the principle line of defense against invading microbes. Antibodies are specific molecules that recognize foreign invaders. These antibodies coat the surface of a group of white blood cells. Each cell carries a different and unique antibody. Each antibody will fit onto a specific and unique foreign invader. When there is a match between the foreign invader and the antibody, the cell is signaled to multiply. The resulting new cells pour antibody into the system, helping it to alert the rest of the immune system to destroy the invader.

The immune system can recognize the foreign invader by the binding between it and the antibody. The system is slow and while it is gearing itself up to fight the foreign body, the microbe may already be doing damage to the host. There is a constant race between the microbe and the immune system. Often the immune system wins and the host recovers from the effects of the microbe. Further, the host is now protected from reinvasion from this microbe. The host now has an immune system that is "primed" and ready for a second invasion of that specific invader. The immunity of the host to reinfection is the basis for the theory of vaccination.

Vaccines work by producing an immune response to an inactive or harmless form of the microbe and, as a result, creating memory. Upon reinfection, the immune system is primed and ready to respond quickly to the invader. Smallpox was eradicated because of the successful use of vaccines. The vaccines used in the 1960's and 1970's were similar to the original vaccine of Jenner. The vaccines were a harmless form of the smallpox virus. This harmless virus primed the immune systems of those who had received the vaccine and rendered them immune to infection by the deadly virus. The smallpox virus was virtually eradicated by 1979 when it only remained in the laboratories of scientists. Smallpox was deadly because it won the race between itself and the host's immune system almost every time. But when it encountered a primed immune system ready for infection, it had no option but to succumb to the host's immune system and be destroyed.

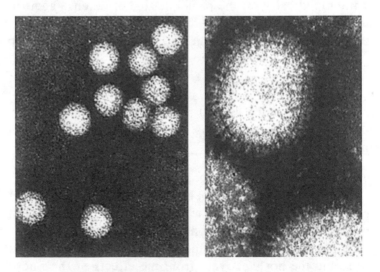

New strains of the influenza virus appear each year and new vaccines must be found.

The Flu

Unfortunately, the flu virus is more versatile than the smallpox virus. The flu virus still poses a deadly threat to the world's population. It is constantly changing into new and different forms. The body's immune system is kept off guard, because it does not recognize the new, changed virus. From year to year, new strains of the virus appear and new vaccine must be made. The vaccines that worked in previous years may not be successful this year.

Dr. Nancy Cox is the head of the CDC's Influenza Branch. It is her responsibility to choose which vaccines are made for each year. Only three strains of flu can be vaccinated against at one time. The potential candidates that may cause the next flu epidemic are sent to Dr. Cox each year. Flu viruses arrive from all over the world. Her position is difficult and filled with constant pressure. Each virus is a potential candidate to be used in the new vaccine and must be tested rigorously in a short period of time. Dr. Cox must anticipate what flu viruses to include in the vaccine to be used the following winter. The decision must be made by spring so the vaccine manufacturers have time to make the appropriate number of doses. The total time in which Dr. Cox and her colleagues must do their jobs is a few weeks.

Viral Strains

There are two types of virus, Type A and Type B. Each year one type of virus dominates, either A or B. Strains are named for the region or country in which it was found. This particular year, the B–type seems to dominate. However, there are viruses from Brazil and China that do not react to the antibodies produced by the current vaccine to B–Panama.

Scientists fear that because there is a large amount of B–type virus circulating, there may be a B–type epidemic in the coming season. The virus found in China is of great concern. The Chinese virus is a B–type and causes severe flu cases. This virus is named Guandong after the province it was found in. To find out if the B–Guandong is different from B–Panama, antibodies which worked successfully against the B–Panama are tested against the B–Guandong virus. Each strain of virus is tested against antibodies made to other viruses. If they crossreact, the vaccine will work against both viral strains. Strains that do not crossreact are watched and their spread monitored carefully. The antibody test indicates that B–Guandong is a new variant. It does not crossreact with the B–Panama antibodies. This suggests B–Guandong is a virus to be monitored carefully.

Viral Structures

The virus itself is coated with spike structures. These spikes are the structures which our antibodies recognize. The virus is able to disguise itself from the immune system by changing the spikes on the cell surface. The genome of the virus contains eight genes and is made up of single–stranded RNA. RNA, or ribonucleic acid, is a molecule that is chemically related to DNA.

Genes are carried in most living organisms in DNA, a relatively stable molecule. However, RNA is highly mutagenic so the influenza genome is constantly changing. A small change in the surface spikes is enough to fool antibodies produced from previous vaccines. These antibodies cannot recognize the new surface spikes, so the virus goes undetected by the old flu antibodies. The ability of influenza virus to change and to elude the immune system, despite the wealth of knowledge that has been accumulated about the virus, is fascinating. Researchers liken the experience of guessing what the virus will do next to a puzzle.

Differences in Viral Structure

The CDC stores samples of influenza virus. In these archives are all the influenza viruses discovered, including the viruses that caused the great epidemics of the past. The differences between many of these viruses are in their surface spikes. Computer programs show that small differences in the protein chain making up the spikes can cause large differences in the physical structure of the spikes.

It is Dr. Cox's responsibility to choose the three strains of virus that will, in her opinion, cause the most damage each year and use these strains to produce vaccines. The question for this year is whether Dr. Cox will choose B–Guandong to be one of the viruses included in this year's mix. Cox also studies the spread of the different viruses. B–Guandong has spread to Taiwan, Cambodia, Australia, Chile, Argentina, and Brazil. The spread of the virus is an indicator to Dr. Cox that the virus may be a candidate for a vaccine. The decision Cox must make is complex and based on many indicators. Whether or not the flu vaccine is successful depends on her decision. Only time can tell whether she has made the right choices.

Changes in the virus caused pandemics in 1918, 1957, and 1968. The virus had completely changed its look each time there was an epidemic. The epidemic in 1957 was called the Asian flu, while the 1968 epidemic was called the Hong Kong flu. Prior to the Hong Kong flu pandemic, scientists believed the influenza virus changed slowly through time until it had accumulated many changes. The changes in the virus after 1968 were too great to be accounted for by an accumulation of changes. The surface spikes looked totally different. Around the same time there had been cases of influenza reported in other organisms, including horses, chickens, and pigs. It was at this point the search began for a source that could account for the huge changes in the spikes of the Hong Kong flu. The surface proteins involved in the 1968 Hong Kong flu pandemic were the same as those found in ducks in Canada. In fact, two genes were identical.

Carrier Ducks

This finding was interesting because the Canadian ducks do not have the disease although they carry the virus. The virus is passed from duck to duck through the water they swim in. However, ducks cannot transmit the virus to humans. Humans cannot get the disease, for instance, by eating the meat of the duck. Eventually, the Hong Kong virus was found to have three of the eight genes from the Canadian duck virus. In addition, the observation was made that most of the epidemics of influenza virus originated in China or Southeast Asia. Therefore, scientists had these two pieces of information to work with: an influenza virus sharing three of eight genes with the Canadian duck virus and epidemics which began in Asia. The next step for scientists was to put each of these pieces of infor-

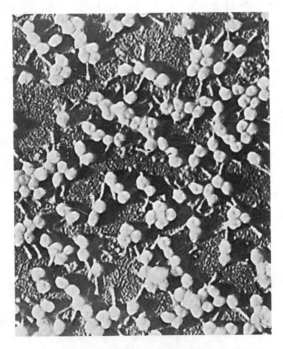

A new influenza virus can develop from the combination of other flu viruses.

mation together to make a workable theory. The association was made while observing the living conditions in Southeast Asia and China.

Families making their living by farming do so on very little land. On this land, pigs and ducks also keep very close quarters. The pig can play host to both the human and duck viruses. It was the pig that was the mixing ground for the two viruses. Genes from these two viruses were able to mix and exchange information. A new and radically different human influenza virus was born from this exchange.

The immune system of newly infected individuals did not recognize the virus and although they did eventually mount an immune response, it was not fast enough. As a result, the new virus became harmful to its host. There were no available vaccines for these new strains. Since it takes manufacturers time to make new vaccines, there was no immune defense and the virus spread rapidly throughout the world. It is the job of the CDC to constantly look for potentially pandemic strains of the influenza virus and new variants that should be included in the new vaccines.

The farming situation in rural China and Southeast Asia has not changed. Because of this, the question for scientists is not if there will be another sudden change in the influenza virus that could cause a pandemic, but rather when. The influenza virus will never be eradicated in the same way smallpox was. This is due to the constant changes the influenza virus undergoes over time. Scientists are content to be one step ahead of the virus.

Schistosomiasis

Another type of microbe able to infiltrate our immune system is Schistosomiasis. Schistosomiasis is a parasitic disease which fools the body into believing the parasite is "self" or human in origin. There is no vaccine for this microbe. Four hundred years ago, Portuguese colonists brought a new disease to Brazil. This disease not only affected the native population, but also the colonists who introduced the disease. The disease has devastated millions since that time. Eight to ten million individuals are affected in Brazil, about 1/20 of the total affected by the parasite worldwide. Don Harn, his associate from the Harvard University School of Public Health, Evan Secor, and Brazilian biologist Mitermeyer Reis are working together to develop a vaccine for this disease. They do much of their work in a Brazilian town called Itaquara. A lagoon was created in this town by damming the stream that runs through it. The lagoon is a valued asset, but at the same time it is a breeding ground for the Schistosomiasis parasite.

Life Cycle of Schistosomiasis

Schistosomiasis spends part of its life cycle in freshwater snails. These snails live in the lagoon and use human waste as a food source. Larvae live inside the snail but are triggered by sunlight to leave the host. The larvae swim freely in this freshwater lagoon, seeking human hosts. The larvae are 1/8 of an inch in length and enter their human hosts via the skin. In the human host, the larvae mature in the veins of the intestine into one–inch–long adult worms. The male and female forms mate permanently and produce eggs. The life span of the adult worm can be as long as 20 years. In that time the female can produce billions of eggs. The eggs cause inflammation of the liver and distended abdomens. Eggs are excreted by the human host and these eggs find their way back into the water supply where they find their new host, the freshwater snail. The life cycle is now complete.

Some obvious ways to combat the disease are through education and improvement of sanitary conditions. Often this is not enough to prevent the spread of disease. Dr. Reis believes that if the people of Itaquara were given latrines and taught the importance of using them, the transmission of the disease should be diminished. Upon visiting the town, the group decided the lagoon is too central to the townspeople's existence. They conclude education and sanitation will not be enough to stop the Schistosomiasis infection cycle.

Dr. Harn began his quest for a vaccine over ten years ago. At this time he was touring a town in Brazil similar to Itaquara. The town had been given all the information and education about the disease, but it did not break the cycle of infection. While there are drugs that are often effective in treating the Schistosomiasis–related infections, multiple infections can cause greater damage and lead to death.

The Schistosomiasis' Disguise

The Schistosomiasis parasite evades the immune system. The adult worm can be an inch long but still not recognized by the immune system. The worm has surface proteins which label the or-

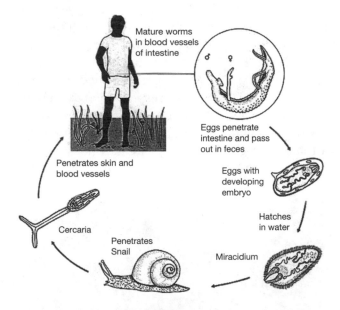

The life cycle of the Schistosomiasis, a parasitic worm. Scientists are currently working on a vaccine for Schistosomiasis.

ganism as foreign. These surface proteins can elicit an immune response and work in much the same way as the spikes on the influenza virus. The secret is the parasite is able to hide itself from the host's immune system. Harn would like to create a vaccine to Schistosomiasis' larval stage.

If this could be accomplished, the immune system would recognize the larvae when they invade and before they mature into egg–laying adults. The vaccine must work on the larvae before they acquire the human disguise. For a vaccine of this type to work, the immune system must recognize the larvae stage as foreign invaders. Harn and his colleagues collected 300 blood samples from different individuals who live in Itaquara.

The immune or white cells are separated from the rest of the blood cells. The white blood cells contain T–cells. The scientists would like to measure the T–cell reaction to the antigens isolated from the Schistosomiasis larvae.

Presently there are two surface proteins or antigens that have been tested against white blood cells from affected individuals. The test is called the proliferation assay and takes a total of five days. In that time, the white blood cells are incubated with the antigens. The immune cells or T–cells have responded extremely well to the Schistosomiasis antigens. Therefore, these antigens are good candidates for the production of vaccines. There is still a long path to travel to translate these laboratory results into a successful vaccine.

Human Gene Therapy

History is Made

Gene therapy is a treatment for genetic disease that replaces the defective gene. Dr. French Anderson, a researcher at the NIH, has been debating whether the time is right for attempting genetic therapies for diseases. Dr. Anderson found that most responses to his ideas were that his basis was unsound and premature. He was accused of "headline grabbing" and attempting to try something that society, at present, was not ready for and would not be ready until at least a decade or more had passed.

In 1992, the first genetic therapy human trial began. A young girl from Cleveland, Ohio is one of 25 individuals known to be affected with a genetic disease of her immune system. She was the first person to be treated by gene therapy at the National Institutes of Health.

The treatment is experimental. No one knows how a human being will react to changing and manipulating its genetic component. This was all explained to the young girl and her family. Their decision was to accept the risk and to go ahead with the treatment because this treatment was their last hope for a normal healthy child.

The girl's condition began as an infant. She suffered from infection after infection as an infant. After the first year and a half she was essentially quarantined from the outside world and potentially infectious and deadly microbes. She was kept at home and away from other children. The only time she left the house was when she went to visit her physician.

It was their physician who first suggested her disease could be potentially treated by gene therapy. However, at the time, the physician thought that route would not be possible for years and years to come. It became a reality much sooner.

According to Dr. Anderson there was a large "emotional resistance" to the first gene therapy experiment such that it took almost four years to gain the necessary permissions to proceed with such a controversial procedure. This was an important beginning for modern medicine and gene therapy. If the therapy were to fail miserably, then the whole field would be set back. Dr. Anderson had to anticipate every mistake. His method, by which the normal gene would replace the mutant gene, was a controversial choice. Anderson chose a virus which causes cancer in mice to be the vehicle on which the normal gene would be transported to the young girl's DNA.

A Healing Virus?

In the mouse, the virus injects its lethal genes into the cells. These viral genes become incorporated into the mouse DNA and cause the cell to become malignant. The result would be cancer growth. The virus had to be altered so it would not cause cancer, but transfer normal genes for abnormal genes. The cancer–causing viral genes were deleted from the viral DNA and the normal gene was inserted in its place. Then the patient would have to be in-

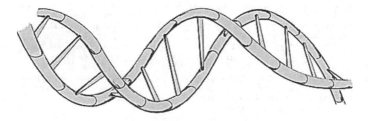

DNA is often manipulated to test scientific theories.

fected with the virus, which would insert its DNA in the genome as if it were carrying the cancer DNA.

However, the genetically engineered viral DNA contains the normal gene and, as a result, the normal gene is delivered to the cell instead of the cancer–causing DNA. Once delivered, the virus must replace the defective gene with the normal one. It does this by the same mechanism that the cancer–causing DNA is incorporated into the host cell's DNA. However, instead of the cancer–causing genes being inserted into the host's DNA, the normal gene is inserted. The effects of gene therapy on human patients are not known and there are risks involved with this method of gene therapy. The virus must insert its DNA into the host's genome. If this insertion occurs in a vital gene, then the results could be deleterious to the host.

Dr. Anderson needed, as a test of his procedure, a disease caused by a mutation in a gene. This mutation would need to result in a disease not treatable by any known medical procedure. The disease also had to be deadly enough to warrant genetic therapy. The disease chosen for the first experiments in human gene therapy was an immune disease which caused the immune system not to work at all. The disease is the "baby in the bubble" disease. Persons affected by this disease must be isolated from all sources of infection. The genetic defect is in the gene encoding for the enzyme ADA. Anderson wanted to give babies that suffered from this disease a single copy of the normal gene. Dr. Anderson published his findings in a review article in a reputable journal, *Science*, in 1984. At the time, however, many people disagreed with the method and the disease which he chose. One of the questions was which cells should receive a copy of the normal gene. The obvious answer is the cells of the immune system, however, neither Dr. Anderson nor anyone else could find a good source of these cells.

Kevin Culver and Michael Blaese were immunologists who collaborated with Dr. Anderson on his project. The cells which Dr. Culver and Dr. Blaese suggested using were white blood cells. These cells are mature cells of the immune system which circulate in the bloodstream. The therapy will only be temporary because imma- ture cells will grow and replace the mature cells. However, even if the effect was temporary, the theory would have been proved cor- rect and the babies should be positively affected by the presence of the normal gene. While Dr. Anderson's ideas were being refined and criticized, a new treatment was devised for children suffering from this disease. However, Dr. Anderson's patient did not respond well to this new medication and her family began discussions with the group at the National Institutes of Health on the possibility of genetic therapy. Since the experimental procedure had never been done on humans before, the girl's family was worried about the consequences and risks of the treatment.

The Controversy Begins

The National Institutes of Health set up a special committee to debate the controversial therapy that Dr. Anderson was proposing. Dr. Robert F. Murray, Jr., from Howard University in Washington, D.C., was concerned about the public's response to gene therapy. He believed people think that by altering a person's genes, the whole form of the person can change. He recalled science fiction stories of mutant frogs, giant insects, giant human beings, etc., all the result of scientific experiments gone awry. This can be frightening to people. The first step, he thought, was to change the way people view these things, to change their attitudes. Dr. Anderson spent many years laying the groundwork, not only scientific but also political, so that gene therapy could become a reality.

On July 31, 1990, Peter Jennings announced on *"World News To- night"* that "the stuff of science fiction was about to become sci- ence fact." This was the day the government committee finally ap- proved Dr. Anderson's proposal for the first experimental genetic therapy. Dr. Anderson knew this was the first step in what would be a revolution in modern medicine and the treatment of genetic dis- ease. The following day, the girl's family signed formal permission forms to begin the clinical trial and the treatment began later that day.

First, the immune cells, harvested from the child earlier and treated with the virus, were returned to her circulatory system. The first few treatments did not show any effects. However, soon after, the entire family came down with the flu. The family was surprised when the girl was the first to recover from the infection. After that episode, the family noticed the girl did not have a running nose all the time, she was not always irritable and her behavior had improved. However, she still continues to return to the National Institutes of Health since the effect of the treatments are not permanent. She has been treated a total of nine times so far and has shown progress in her ability to fight infection.

Now the young girl does not stay at home all the time anymore. She visits public places without fear of contracting infections, but her health is still a primary concern of her parents. A permanent cure would be to replace the mutant gene in the stem cell of the immune system. The stem cell is the immature cell from which all cells in the immune system are derived. There has been continued success in locating these stem cells.

The success of the first genetic therapy has opened the door for new therapies. Dr. Culver thinks of the contribution made by himself and Dr. Anderson's group as one of opening doors for new frontiers in modern medicine and genetic therapies. Also, people's attitudes toward science are changing. Culver believes that their first patient, a sweet four–year–old little girl who is now able to play in the park with other children, has replaced the genetic monster of science fiction in the minds of the public. And it is because of gene therapy that a little girl is cured of her debilitating genetic disease.

There have been dozens of therapies initiated since this first therapy, including some for such diseases as cancer and heart conditions. However, not all genetic diseases lend themselves well to this type of therapy and the therapies themselves are very expensive.

A Cure for Cystic Fibrosis?

For example, the mutant gene cannot be replaced in patients with cystic fibrosis. Lung cells cannot be removed, treated, and then transplanted back into the patient. Scientists continue to struggle with new approaches to therapies. Ron Crystal, of the National Institutes of Health, continues to attempt new methods for gene therapy in cystic fibrosis. Dr. Crystal likens the lung to a large tree with many branches. It is impossible to remove. The only way to treat the cells of the lung is to treat the cells while they are still in the patient. Some cystic fibrosis patients can live past their teens and 20's. One such patient is 42 years old, but needs constant medical attention. His lungs cannot secrete fluid normally, which results in the accumulation of mucus in the lung. This mucus is a breeding ground for infectious microbes.

The adenovirus is the microbe responsible for the common cold. The virus is able to deliver its viral genes to the cells in the lung. It may be a good candidate for delivering the normal genes to the lining of the lung. Dr. Crystal has taken out the infectious genes of the adenovirus and replaced them with the normal cystic fibrosis gene. He believes the virus should then carry the normal copies of the genes to the cells in the lining of the lung. The virus should invade these cells as it would normally during an infection. However, these adenovirus have been manipulated to contain the normal cystic fibrosis genes.

The adenovirus does not insert its gene into the chromosome. Preliminary experiments in tissue culture cells indicate adenovirus, engineered with normal genes, can express the gene products in cystic fibrosis cells and can effectively cure them. This therapy had to be tested in tissue culture before it could be used in clinical trials or even be considered for gene therapy. Tissue culture cells were used because there is, at present, no animal model for cystic fibrosis. In tissue culture, the cells from the cystic fibrosis patient are stained purple in color.

The Adenovirus

The adenovirus is added to the cultured cells. As the adenovirus delivered the normal genes to these cells, the color changed to yellow. When the cells are functioning normally, the cells turn red. Dr. Crystal believes the adenovirus will deliver the correct gene to the cells lining the lung. He also believes that delivering the gene will be an effective biological cure for cystic fibrosis. The question remaining is how safe will it be? Delivery of adenovirus may be achieved by aerosol spray. What the risks are to the patient is, again, unknown. Dr. Crystal envisions a patient being able to breathe air containing the cure for their disease. Families with cystic fibrosis–afflicted children are waiting anxiously for a cure. Many see it as a race between the progressive nature of cystic fibrosis and technology.

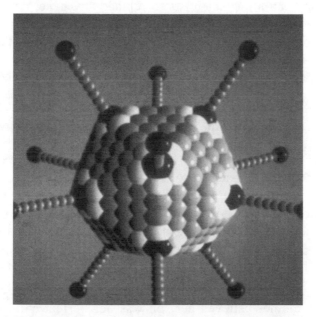

The adenovirus is a microbe which is able to deliver viral genes to the lungs. It may be useful in fighting Cystic Fibrosis.

Dr. Anderson's initial results have opened the gate for new approaches and methods. He hopes that one day a cure will be as simple as an injection of a therapeutic gene. Years ago this was the stuff of science fiction. *Fantastic Voyage*, a film made in 1966, is an example of this. In the film, a submarine and its crew are miniaturized and injected into a patient to travel to the place of injury and perform the appropriate treatment. The hope is for a universal delivery system which would be used in all genetic therapies. Dr. Anderson's vision of the future does not involve a miniature submarine, but rather a therapy where a gene can be delivered anywhere in the body at any time.

The Future

Gene therapies are envisioned as cures for genetic disease, but technology can allow scientists to replace any gene, defective or not. For example, skin color could change according to the preference of the patient. Many researchers are not pleased as they look down the road to the future of genetic technology. Another example is intelligence. What would happen if a gene was found that could increase intelligence? Would people want to give these genes to their children, to themselves? Now that science fiction is science fact, how will human beings handle this newfound power?

Gene therapy is currently being used to cure genetic diseases because they are considered to be "bad" by society. With this new technology, will the definition of "bad" genes change? For example, growth hormones are now routinely used to treat short people even though they were intended for individuals affected with a specific growth–stunting condition. The growth hormone treatments are being used for cosmetic purposes.

Every parent wants their child to be perfect, healthy, and normal. One mother believed her son was her perfect child until he stopped growing. His friends continued to grow and were becoming faster, stronger, and bigger. The boy's projected adult height was 5 foot 2 inches, but the doctors could not guarantee he would reach that height. His mother then began to seek alternate treatments for his condition.

He is now treated with daily injections of growth hormone and must visit his doctor every three months. He is growing more quickly and is no longer short for his age. Both his doctor and his mother keep close track of his progress. However, one can ask, what was wrong with his being short?

Society's Definition of "Normal"

His mother believed that society has certain attitudes toward people who do not fall into their definition of normal. She simply did not want her son to live his life being different and outside the norm. She did not want her son stigmatized because he was short.

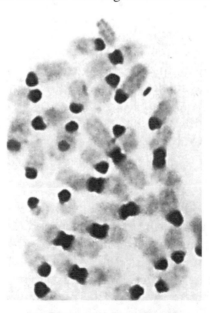

Manipulating chromosomes through gene therapy is being used to cure many types of genetic diseases.

She does wonder if he would have ever noticed he was short if she had not pointed it out. However, when she heard of the growth hormone treatment she jumped at the chance. In addition, treatment with growth hormone has few side effects. As a result of the treatment, he has grown two to three inches in one year. She believes he is more confident and feels better about himself as a person. She also believes she is doing what is best for her son. Ultimately, hormone therapy has allowed him to reshape himself. Genetic therapy may some day enable individuals to do this on a larger scale. Although growth hormone was first manufactured to treat persons of short stature, the public response was immediate. There was a flood of calls from parents who wanted their children to be above average so they could excel in basketball or other athletic competitions.

Many doctors believe this use goes beyond the medical and ethical use of the hormone. They believe the result of this type of treatment is to treat vanity, not a medical illness. An individual's desires to be bigger and better are extensions of natural instinct and human beings appear to have an instinct to be one–better than the next person. If this is the case, then being taller than average is considered to be advantageous. Then a short person, although height doesn't make you a better person, wants, because of instinct, to be taller. People will wear elevator shoes or take growth hormones, whatever works, whatever makes them taller. Some believe there is a "pecking order" in our genetic material and to overcome these attitudes will be difficult.

It has taken 3.5 billion years for nature to create, by evolution, a human being. Using current technology, scientists and doctors can change our genetic makeup in a matter of hours, days, weeks, or years. Just over the genetic horizon is the ability to cure embryos of their genetic defects before they are even born. Now that the technology is here to change the genetic makeup of individuals, where will it lead us? Where will scientists start and stop altering a person's DNA?

The Problems of Genetic Conformity

If people can be genetically cured of their diseases, they will pass on the normal copies of their genes, and not the abnormal genes, to future generations. If this is the case, then entire mutant genes could be deleted from populations. Would this lead to genetic conformity and is this good for the human race? As we have seen earlier, diversity is the key to surviving. Will genetic engineering make human beings more genetically identical and, therefore, reduce the fitness of the species as a whole? Will genetics become the fashion? Instead of designer clothes, will they be replaced by designer genes? Will society force families with genetic defects to correct them? Even if it is against their will? Will humans learn from past experience? Whenever humans have conquered one of nature's secrets, humans have made many mistakes. Will we make the same mistakes as we venture into the brave new world of genetic engineering? This time, however, humans are tinkering with DNA, the very stuff that makes them human. This time the stakes seem higher. Genetic engineering allows us to change who we are. With this type of power, there is no room for mistakes.

DNA and Behavior

Shaping Personality

Every individual is different. Even identical twins have different personality traits. The main idea behind the biological revolution is that DNA is involved in forming individuals. What role do genes play in determining individuality and personality? Is personality predetermined in the genes and formed long before childhood? Or are childhood experiences important in shaping personality? Do genes determine our employers, our choice of spouses, the timing of romance, our political views? Does DNA contain the information to tell us who will be sociable or shy? A criminal or a law enforcement official?

Scientists are beginning to study DNA's role in individuality. Is it their own DNA that made them scientists? Scientists are not able

Scientists are studying the DNA of identical twins and its role in individuality.

to clone human beings. Nature does when identical twins are born. These individuals share the same DNA. There are some who believe it is our genes, not the environment, making us who we are. By this way of thinking, identical individuals, regardless of the environment in which they were raised, would be the same.

The role DNA plays in shaping the personality of an individual is being investigated by scientists studying identical twins. Identical twins are exact copies of each other, down to their DNA. Fraternal twins, twins coming from different eggs, share 50% of their DNA. Once a year, in Twinsburg, Ohio, there is a Twins' Day Festival. Here, thousands of twins gather from all over the world.

Twin Studies

Dr. Lindon Eaves, of Virginia Commonwealth University, uses this opportunity to study a large number of twins. He is interested in personalities, lifestyles, and social attitudes. These types of qualities, that define individuality, make us human. Questionnaires are used that twins, both fraternal and identical, and their families fill out. The topics on the questionnaires were chosen deliberately to reflect these characteristics. Persons who fill out the questionnaire are asked to agree, disagree, or neither to 28 different topics. The topics cover a wide range of issues, from astrology to X–rated movies.

When the results are tallied, it is found that identical twins answer similarly more often then fraternal twins, perhaps because they share more genetic similarity than fraternal twins. Genes do determine differences between humans. Professor Eaves believes for the past 50 years humans have tended to believe these differences were due to social circumstance rather than genes.

These differences between human beings were used as rationalization for the Japanese–American internment camps in the United States and Canada during World War II. Regardless of citizenship or birthplace, individuals were considered dangerous and suspect because of their ancestry, their genes. The military officials in charge of the internment of the Japanese in the United States believed the behavior was in the blood.

The same arguments were being made in Europe, where racism was used as an excuse for concentration camps where gypsies, mentally disabled individuals, homosexuals, and Jews were exterminated in the Holocaust. The Nazis believed the genes of the Aryan race were superior to those of all other races. The doctrine of racial purity was used as rationalization for sterilization, enslavement, and murder.

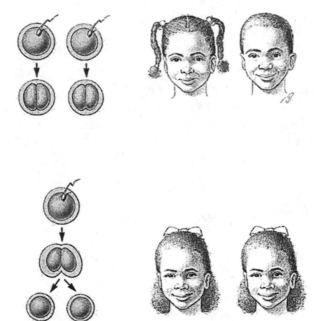

Fraternal and identical twins are studied to determine how similar their beliefs, views, and opinions are.

The theory that bad genes could be bred out of the human race was the basis of the Eugenics Movement, the popular view of genetics during the 1920's and 1930's. The Eugenics Movement also believed good traits could be bred into humans. This popular view of genetics was the basis for the atrocities of World War II and, because of the outcome of such attitudes, Eugenics has fallen out of favor as a socially acceptable ideal. The pendulum now reversed direction and the environment has become the primary focus as the force shaping personality. The environment plays an important role in shaping individuals and it is this role that society has emphasized. However, the role of genes in personality has come back into the spotlight.

Observation and Learning

The fruit fly is an organism in which programmed responses can be studied. Much is known about the genetics of fruit flies but only recently have scientists like Tim Tully, of Cold Spring Harbor Laboratory, become interested in the relationship between genes and behavior. Originally the fly's behavior was described as a series of programmed and instinctive responses. However, Dr. Tully has discovered that patterns of behavior in flies can be a learned experience.

Flies are subjected to a series of odors with and without electric shock. Their ability to remember and learn the association between odor and electric shock is studied. Flies are placed in a "training chamber" that is wired to a source of electricity. There the flies are subjected to an odor called "O". The flies are known to dislike this odor. Simultaneously, the flies are subjected to small electric shocks. The flies are then subjected to another odor they dislike, this one is designated "M". However there are no electric shocks delivered with the odor. When the flies are given a choice of odors, "O" or "M," most of the flies will choose "M" because they have learned to associate the electric shocks with the "O" odor. There are many genes involved in the ability of flies to learn. All these genes are involved in the biochemistry of the brain and Dr. Tully has identified several of them.

The expression of genes determines how the nervous system is interconnected and gives it the ability to respond to environmental stimuli. Another function of genes is to set up the environment within a nerve cell, allowing the cell to respond to environmental signals. Changes in the environment will affect the fitness of an individual. Therefore, it is vital for an organism, in order to survive, to be able to learn about the environment. This ability would give the organism a great advantage in survival. The ability to learn one's environment will be dependent on the individual and will vary between individuals. The genes of the fruit fly allow them to learn and adapt to their environment.

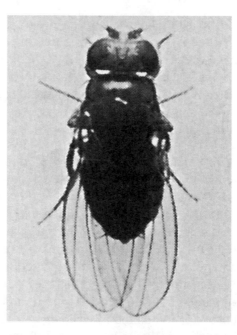

Studies have shown that a fruit fly can be taught to adapt to its environment.

Dogs were domesticated from wolves and have inherited some of the behaviors of their ancestors. In this case, there was a group of wolves with specific genes that allowed them to adapt to a different environment. The change in environment was from living in the wild to living with humans. The modern sheepdog is a direct descendant of the wolf. Instead of exhibiting the behavior for hunting and killing, they have adapted behavior to do something more useful to humans. The ability of some dogs to become domesticated was not as simple as breeding out the "hunting" and "killing" genes and breeding in the "herding" genes. Dog owners will testify that good working dogs have an instinct for their work. This instinct is a behavior programmed by genes. If a dog possesses this instinct, it can then learn, with training, to use this instinct.

Learned vs. Instinctive Behavior

For instance, some dog trainers can tell if a sheepdog puppy will be a good herder by observing his instinctive behavior. Herding is an ancestral behavior, probably associated with the pack hunting behavior of wolves. Working dogs call upon this instinct and then learn to apply it to the herding of sheep and cattle. However, it is not as easy as just having good instincts. The dog must also be trained. About 80% of dogs will show an inclination for work. If they do not show this initial behavior they will never work. The 80% who can work must then be trained properly. The ability of a dog to be trained is based on his instinct, which is programmed in his genes, as well as the ability to learn.

The genes that make good sheepdogs are those which give the dogs flexibility to learn and adapt to different environments. Sheepdogs are not kinder and gentler versions of wolves because the killer genes of their ancestors have been bred out. Rather, the sheepdogs have been bred such that they can take advantage of their ability to learn and adapt to new environments and new behaviors. Without training, many dogs will revert back to their wild nature. If a dog's genes completely controlled their behavior, they would always behave as wolves. There is an important environmental component to behavior. Genes give the brain the ability to react, adapt, and learn in response to environmental cues.

Mice can learn behavior by simply observing the behavior in another animal. These experiments were conducted at the Jackson Laboratory in Bar Harbor, Maine. This facility is home to 2,500 different strains of mice. Each strain is genetically homogenous and exists in identical environmental conditions. Researchers at "Mouse College" are interested in the differences between these many strains of mice.

In one particular experiment, three mice are allowed to observe one mouse, the tutor mouse, while two control mice are not allowed to see the tutor mouse. The tutor mouse must reach a food

Sheepdogs are bred to have "herding genes." This, combined with training and instinct, allow the dogs to adapt to different environments.

reward by opening a swinging door. The swinging door only opens in one direction. After the tutor has been through the obstacle course a few times, the observing mice are allowed to attempt to negotiate the course.

The swinging door is modified to open in either direction. The mice that were able to watch the tutor mouse learn to open the door quickly. Furthermore, they open the door in the same way the tutor mouse did, even though the door could be opened in either direction. The control mice, who did not watch the tutor mouse, take longer to learn the behavior. The control mice also open the door in either direction. The experiment demonstrates mice can learn behavior by observation alone.

Observation is one mechanism by which organisms can learn. This explains why children are so much like their parents. Not only do parents pass on their genes but they also pass on their values and behaviors. Children can learn behaviors by watching their parents. They do not have to experience the behavior to learn it. Observational learning is a critical trait needed for survival in the wild. For example, polar bear cubs stay with their mother two to three years after birth. During that time, the cubs watch and learn from their mother the survival techniques they will need for their own survival. If the behavior is not learned, the cubs will not survive.

Progression of the Species

Evolutionary Stagnation?

As humans gain even more control over their environment, they become increasingly isolated from the very processes that originally brought them into existence. Natural selection and speciation are no longer the major determinants in human evolution as the evolutionary forces on man have dissipated. No longer do humans worry about predators carrying off the weak and unfit. As man has learned to manipulate his own environment, he has become insulated from the forces that drive evolution. Developments in medicine and technology have eliminated most of the inherited genetic

The world is filled with genetically diverse people.

diseases that also served as a method to select for survival of the fittest. Because of these advances, most people today survive to the age of reproduction and, as we have seen earlier, reproduction is the ultimate determinant of fitness. Therefore, in evolutionary terms, today almost everyone is fit.

The elimination of population isolation because of the breakdown of geographical barriers and the intermixing of different populations has weakened the forces that drive evolution. Isolated populations serve as a testing ground for new genetic adaptations, which, if they are beneficial to the organism, survive. Eventually, if these adaptations are successful enough, they result in a new species. As the human gene pool becomes increasingly homogenous, opportunity for genetic adaptation is abated. Unfortunately, like the Eugenics Movement of the 1920's, this argument can be translated into a call for ethnic "purity," ignoring the fact that the term "isolated populations" does not specify race or ethnicity. Any population, racially diverse or otherwise, would be a testing ground for genetic adaptations if they were isolated from all other populations. However, in our emerging global culture, this has become highly unlikely.

The combination of these factors has suggested to some scientists that human evolution is coming to an end. They postulate that humans will enter a period of evolutionary status quo and will thus remain largely unchanged in the foreseeable future. Many scientists, such as Dr. Steve Jones at the University College of London, believe that the evolution of the human species is complete and will become a "living fossil." But instead of facing extinction, we will reshape the environment in order to survive. However, with the reshaping of the environment comes the risk of the destruction of natural habitats and also the possibility of an increase in pollution. Both changes can result in severe climatic fluctuations.

Climatic changes are a major evolutionary force that could ultimately have a devastating effect on all life, not only human. However, barring any unforeseen climatic catastrophe, is humankind resigned to evolutionary stagnation or will it take evolution into its own hands and, through the use of genetic engineering, map his own future?

The question of whether or not humans should tinker with their own genetic makeup in an attempt to guide the course of evolution is both an ethical and political one. It is also a dilemma that will not be resolved anytime in the near future.

The Shaping of an Individual

There are many genes associated with behavior, but the genetic component is not the sole determinant in behavior. Scientific claims that propose a purely genetic component in behaviors such as criminality or intelligence are false. Knowing the exact sequence of an individual's genome will not predict that individual's personality. The environment must also be taken into consideration. However, even taking into consideration both genetic and environmental components may not tell you the whole story with regard to personality.

Many researchers believe that some genetic traits may be due to pure chance and the same genes may react differently in different individuals, even if they are in the same environment. Twin studies seem to bear out this hypothesis. Human identical twins are genetically identical and share the same environment, but have distinctly different personality traits.

Whether genes, environment, or both are involved in personality, the important factor is that human beings believe they themselves have control over personality and their own destiny. Perhaps the best way to describe behavior in humans is freedom of choice. The underlying theme of social and religious institutions is that humans can make choices and are held responsible for the choices they make.

Science is not telling us that humans are genetically preprogrammed robots with no freedom or will to choose. Rather, it is telling us the opposite. The choices that humans make are not only mysteries of science but can also be a mystery to the individual. DNA created the complex organ called the brain, which in turn created abstract and complex ideas, such as language and technology. These complex processes are those that now allow us to understand and study DNA, the molecule that started the entire process. Genes alone do not determine the choices individuals make in their lifetime. These complex issues involve more than just genes. Experience, environment, and sometimes luck are also important pieces in this puzzle. Humans are influenced by their genetic makeup, but are not dominated by it. In effect, the reason that people have the ability to reproduce, evolve, make choices, develop exciting new technologies, conquer disease, and shape their own destinies is because DNA has given us the capability.

CHAPTER 1

Cell Mechanics

When a cell divides, its daughter cells must have the appropriate genetic material. For mitosis, two daughter nuclei are produced that have the same number and type of chromosomes as the parent nucleus. If the parent cell is **haploid** (contains only one of each chromosome), then the daughter nuclei will also be haploid. Likewise, if the parent cell is **diploid** (contains two copies of each chromosome), the daughter nuclei will also be diploid. For meiosis, the diploid chromosome number is reduced by one-half, producing nuclei that are haploid.

An understanding of the mechanics of cell division depends upon a clear concept of the chromosome. Its elongated structure contains a single molecule of DNA and a condensed region, a **centromere**. The DNA may be uncoiled, making the chromosome indistinct in appearance, or coiled, making it readily visible. Chromosomes are only visible during mitosis or meiosis.

While interphase chromosomes are not visible, they nonetheless undergo replication, producing two molecules of DNA. It is important to remember that a replicated chromosome contains twice the genetic material, but is still defined as a single chromosome. The two DNA molecules, called **chromatids**, are held together at their centromeres. Retaining the chromatids as a single chromosome allows for their orderly movement to the equatorial plane of metaphase. To determine the number of chromatids in a dividing cell, double the number of chromosomes present.

The visible stages of cell division (prophase, metaphase, anaphase, and telophase) serve to deliver chromosomes to daughter nuclei. When studying chromosome movement, keep in mind that they do not actively move. Their condensation during prophase allows for easier movement through the cell. Spindle fiber attachment to centromeres and **centrioles** (animal cell) or **poles** (plant cell) provides the means for chromosome movement by lengthening and shortening. Organizing the chromosomes on the equatorial plane ensures that the new cells receive one of each kind of chromosome or homologue.

Understanding the concept of homologous chromosomes helps explain the difference between mitotic and meiotic metaphase organization. **Homologous chromosomes**, chromosomes containing genes for the same characteristics, are found in diploid cells. Remember that each replicated homologue contains identical copies, called chromatids. Therefore, after replication, diploid cells contain homologous pairs of chromosomes, each made of two identical chromatids.

During mitosis, identical chromatids separate, becoming chromosomes. Since chromatids are held together, the chromosomes can line up in any order during metaphase. Each daughter nucleus will receive one copy of each homologue when the chromatids separate.

Meiosis produces haploid cells, so that the diploid number can be restored when fertilization occurs. Therefore, each haploid cell receives only one member of the homologous pairs. Homologous chromosomes first pair as a means of organizing; paired homologues each contain two chromatids, forming the tetrad characteristic of prophase I and metaphase I. The homologous pairs, with their chromatids still attached, separate during the first meiotic division, producing two haploid cells. The second meiotic division merely separates the identical chromatids of each homologue, resulting in a total of four haploid cells. Defining a cell as haploid or diploid depends upon the number of chromosome sets present, regardless of whether the chromosomes exist in their unreplicated form or their chromatid form.

To appreciate the unique features of meiosis, we must understand that sexual reproduction is a means of providing genetic variability. The pairing of homologous chromosomes during prophase I allows for frequent crossing over, as evidenced by the presence of chiasma. Therefore, new combinations of genes appear on the same chromosome. Also, when homologous pairs line up during metaphase I, each homologue has an equal chance of attaching to either pole. Thus, there are $2n$ possible combinations of chromosomes for each gamete produced.

When chromatids (or homologues in meiosis I) fail to separate, abnormal chromosome numbers appear in the daughter nuclei, a process known as **nondisjunction**. To determine the chromosome number caused by nondisjunction, draw the chromosomes as they appear during metaphase, then as they move to the poles. For each nondisjunction, one cell gains a chromosome and the other loses one.

Thus far we have dealt with nuclear events. During mitosis, the cytoplasm usually divides and, in most cases, divides equally. During meiosis, cytoplasmic division is different for sperm production than it is for oocyte production. To appreciate this difference, the role of the sperm and oocyte in sexual reproduction must be understood. Fertilization requires that sperm travel to the ovum, a somewhat hazardous venture. With frequent meiosis and equal cytoplasmic division, large numbers of sperm with sufficient energy sources are provided. Oocyte production involves unequal cytoplasmic division, in order that one of the haploid cells may receive as much cytoplasm as possible. Maximum nutrient and energy sources best support development of the fertilized egg. The other haploid end products of oogenesis, the polar bodies, package and dispose of the extra chromosome sets.

Problem Solving Examples:

Mitosis

 Colchicine blocks mitosis. What does this reveal about the mitotic process?

 The use of drugs with known biochemical targets reveals much about the chemical makeup of biological systems. Colchicine is a drug that causes the dissociation of microtubule polymers into its component subunits. Since colchicine effectively stops mitosis, microtubules must be involved in the mitotic process. Since microtubules are long filamentous polymers, it follows that they make up some long fibrous structure in the mitotic cell. Spindle fibers fit this description perfectly. Experiments using protein extraction techniques, in which fluorescent antibodies are sent to specific microtubule proteins, such as tubulin, and colchicine inhibition have confirmed that microtubules are the major component of spindle fibers.

Meiosis

 Differentiate between continuous fibers, kinetochore (or chromosomal) fibers, neocentric fibers and astral fibers.

 All of these fibers make up the broad category of spindle fibers. Continuous fibers run from pole to pole. These fibers may cause elongation of the spindle during anaphase. Kinetochore fibers, as their name suggests, run from one pole to a kinetochore on a chromosome. These fibers shorten and thus move the chromosomes from the equatorial plane to the poles. Neocentric fibers attach to other parts of the chromosome. Astral fibers radiate from the asters but do not run through the spindle. The differentiation among the various types of fibers indicates that microtubules can vary functionally even though the molecular structure is extremely similar, if not identical.

 What are chiasmata? What important means of genetic exchange are they related to?

Chiasma (the singular form of chiasmata) means a cross. Chiasmata are areas of contact between nonsister chromatids of a meiotic diplonema nucleus which give the chromosomes a crosslike appearance under a light microscope.

Two, three or all four chromatids can participate in chiasma formation and one chromatid can form numerous chiasmata. In normal meiosis, there is at least one chiasma per tetrad.

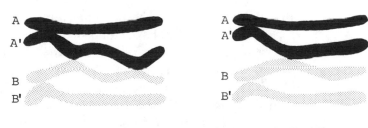

a) One *A′* - *B* chiasma   b) Two *A′* - *B* chiasmata

Figure 1.1

Chiasmata are almost certainly related to crossing over and recombination. There are two sets of experimental data that support this belief. One is that there is a correlation between physical exchange and the occurrence of chiasmata. This was shown from studies of a strain of the plant *Disporum sessile*, which contains easily distinguishable homologous chromosomes called heteromorphic homologues. The other experiment shows a correlation between physical exchange and recombination. This was shown through studies on *Drosophila* strains with mutant X-chromosomes. Neither of these experiments prove that chiasma leads to genetic recombination, but they lend strong support to the hypothesis.

 How does meiosis differ in males and females?

The actual stages of meiosis are the same in males and females. What differs is the time it takes to complete certain stages and the products of the meiotic divisions.

The production of sperm cells by the human male follows the normal meiotic scheme. For each complete round of meiosis, four haploid sperm cells are produced. This meiotic gamete production occurs only after puberty.

In the human female, things are very different. Meiosis begins very early, in the fetus. By birth, all of the potential female sex cells, oocytes, have begun meiosis I, but have stopped at the diplotene stage. They may remain in this state as long as fifty years. When the female reaches sexual maturity the meiosis process continues. Each month, one oocyte resumes meiosis. This meiosis is still dissimilar from that during sperm formation. After meiosis I, the cytoplasm divides unevenly to produce one small cell, a polar body, and one large cell, the oocyte. The polar body may undergo meiosis II to produce two such bodies. The oocyte, meanwhile, enters meiosis II, but it stops again about metaphase II and awaits sperm penetration. Once a sperm has penetrated, the oocyte finishes meiosis II and produces another polar body and a mature haploid egg. When the nuclei of the sperm fuses with that of the egg, the product is a diploid zygote. The polar bodies are usually discarded.

Thus, the meiotic products of male gametogenesis are four sperm cells and those of female gametogenesis are two or three polar bodies and one large oocyte. Since the oocyte must contain a lot of materials to form the initial cells of the developing embryo, it must be very large. The large size of the oocyte is a result of most of the cytoplasm from meiosis going towards the oocyte and very little going towards the remaining three meiotic products. Conversely, sperm do not need to be so large, since their purpose is only to reach the oocyte, to donate their genetic material and to stimulate the oocyte to mature. Thus, the form of meiosis that male and female sex cells undergo is very much determined by their cellular functions.

Haploid and Diploid Number

Q An animal has a diploid number of 8. During meiosis, how many chromatids are present

(a) in the tetrad stage?

(b) in late telophase of the first meiotic division?

(c) in metaphase of the second meiotic division?

 In doing this problem, one must remember that meiosis involves both the duplication of chromosomes and the separation of homologous pairs.

(a) In the tetrad stage of meiosis, homologous chromosomes synapse, or pair. But prior to this, every chromosome had been duplicated. Synapsis therefore results in a tetrad, a bundle of four chromatids (two copies of each one of the homologous chromosomes). The number of tetrads equals the number of haploid chromosomes. Therefore, there are $1/2 \times 8$ or 4 tetrads. Since each tetrad has four chromatids, there are a total of 4×4 or 16 chromatids in the tetrad stage.

(b) In late telophase of the first meiotic division, the homologous chromosomes of each pair have separated. But each chromosome is still double and composed of two daughter chromatids. So there are the haploid number (4) of doubled chromosomes, or a total of 8 chromatids.

(c)   In metaphase of the second meiotic division, the doubled chromosomes have lined up along the equator of the cell, but daughter chromatids have not yet separated. So the number of chromatids is still 4 × 2, or 8.

Variations in Mitosis and Meiosis

Q   The division of dinoflagellates, *Syndinium*, has an unusual variation in its mitotic process. What is the variation? What does it indicate about the evolution of mitosis?

A   Dinoflagellates are unicellular organisms that have two flagella attached laterally. They, along with diatoms, are the primary producers of organic matter in the sea. Their mitotic apparatus is slightly less complex than that of higher eukaryotes.

Throughout the entire cell cycle, the chromosomes remain attached to the microtubules. The microtubules run from the kinetochore to the centriole. The kinetochore is attached to the nuclear membrane, which does not disappear in metaphase. The spindle fibers do not elongate; they act like rigid rods rather than elastic fibers. Thus these organisms have not evolved a separate mechanism for moving their chromosomes via spindle fiber movement.

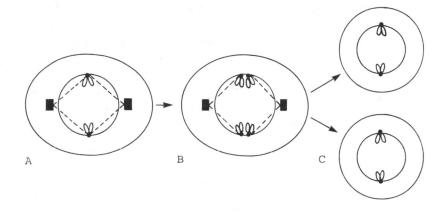

■ = centriole
● = kinetochore
- - - = spindle fiber

Figure 1.2— Mitosis in _Syndinium_

Figure 1.2 shows some of the mitotic steps. In _A_, the chromosomes are attached to both centrioles. When the chromosome appears as sister chromatids, _B_, each kinetochore is attached to one of the centrioles by a microtubule. Each daughter cell, _C_, receives one chromatid from the pair.

This form of mitosis may represent an earlier stage in the evolution of cell division. This is evolutionarily between direct attachment of chromosomes to the membrane and the evolution of the kinetochore as an active chromosome mover. In Syndiniumic mitosis, a separate mechanism for chromosome movement has not evolved.

Q Assuming $2n = 8$, suppose the first meiotic division of a cell is normal, but in one of the two daughter cells nondisjunction of a pair of sister chromatids occurs during the second meiotic division. How many chromatids would be present in each of the four gametes?

A Nondisjunction is occurring in the second meiotic division. This type of nondisjunction results in gametes with different numbers of chromosomes.

From the diagram, nondisjunction during meiosis II results in gametes with 5, 3, 4, and 4 chromatids, respectively.

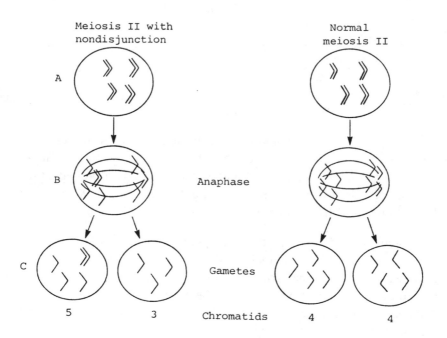

Figure 1.3 — Nondisjunction in the second round of meiosis. Each bent line represents a single chromatid.

CHAPTER 2

Chromosomes

Since chromosomes contain genetic material, it is essential that the correct number and types be present for normal growth and development. During cell division, single DNA molecules coil around major chromosomal components, basic proteins called **histones**. These condensed DNA-histone complexes are visible in the cell as replicated chromosomes, each containing two chromatids. **Karyotypes** (pictures of the cell's chromosomal content organized by length, centromere position, and banding pattern) can be used to determine normal and abnormal chromosome organization and number.

When studying chromosome organization, remember that one chromosome contains one duplex DNA molecule. The linear arrangement of its genes is reflected in the characteristic banding pattern evident when the cell is stained. Changes in chromosome organization, such as duplications, deletions, translocations, and inversions are detectable by examining the banding pattern.

The basis for understanding chromosomal rearrangements is in knowing that chromosomes regularly break, producing sticky ends that are likely to reattach, either restoring the original arrangement or creating any number of rearrangements.

We can analyze the causes and consequences of chromosomal rearrangements by assigning letters in sequence to designated consecutive regions of a chromosome. Uneven crossing over of homologous chromosomes during prophase I of meosis can result in duplication and deficiency. **Inversions** occur when a broken segment flips around and reinserts itself in reverse order. **Translocations** involve the movement of one chromosome or fragment to a nonhomologous chromosome. When chromosome breaks occur, it is possible to predict how reattachments will occur by recombining "sticky" ends in all possible combinations.

When predicting the consequence of a chromosomal rearrangement, pair the normal and abnormal homologs in a diagram so that like regions are next to each other. Attach spindle fibers to the centromeres and draw the resulting chromosomes as they move to the poles. For translocations, the diagram should show the chromosome donating the fragment as well as the recipient chromosome. When translocations occur, it is possible for gametes to get duplications and deletions of genetic material, depending upon how the homologous chromosomes line up.

To predict the consequences of crossing over, indicate the chromosome's position with an *X* and read along one homolog to the *X*, then finish by reading along the other one. If crossing over produces one chromosome with no centromere and another with two, the "centromereless" fragment cannot migrate in the cell and will be lost. In addition, the chromosome containing two centromeres will break as it is pulled to opposite poles during cell division.

The consequences of abnormal chromosome arrangement are determined empirically. Losses of *essential* genetic material result in an abnormal phenotype or failure of a fertilized egg (**zygote**) to develop. Duplications in genetic material may disrupt development (as in Down's syndrome) or create the raw material for evolution, and reorganization of genetic material may affect development if the position of the genes influences their functions.

Abnormal chromosome number may be due to the presence of multiple sets of chromosomes (**euploid**), or an alteration in a portion of a chromosome set (**aneuploid**). Two explanations for euploid — multiple fertilization of an ovum or mitosis without cytokinesis — are more easily understood if diagrammed.

Aneuploids, which are due to nondisjunction, are best visualized by diagramming chromosomes during metaphase of mitosis or meiosis. Attach spindle fibers from centromere to pole and draw the chromosomes as they move poleward. Be sure that one set of chromatids in mitosis or meiosis II, or one pair of homologous chromosomes in meiosis I, do not separate during anaphase, but move to one pole or the other.

The consequences of abnormal chromosome number are also determined empirically. To follow chromosome number through reproduction and development, diagram each stage, showing the chromosome count. Indicate chromosome sets as one set = n (haploid), two sets = $2n$ (diploid), three sets = $3n$ and so on. For aneuploids, designate the addition of a chromosome as +1, of a pair of homologous chromosomes as +2, and the addition of two different chromosomes as +1+1. The loss of chromosomes is indicated by a negative number.

Changes in chromosome number and kind may alter development and viability, as well as provide the raw material for evolution. These changes can be correlated with particular phenotypes.

Problem Solving Examples:

Structure

What are histones ?

Histones are small, basic proteins which bind tightly to the DNA of eukaryotes. The DNA-histone complex is called nucleosome. Histones have a high content of positively charged side chains, especially lysine and arginine residues. A possible mechanism of binding is shown in Figure 2.1. Half of the mass of chromosomes is due to the presence of histones and the remaining mass is from the DNA. Thus, histones are a major component of eukaryotic chromosomes.

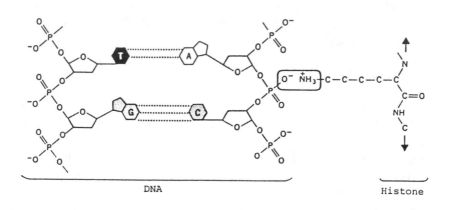

DNA   Histone

Figure 2.1

There are five types of histones: *H*1, *H*2A, *H*2B, *H*3 and *H*4. Each of these types of histones can be modified by methylation, ADP-ribosylation or phosphorylation. These posttranslational modifications may be important in regulating the availability of DNA for replication and transcription by changing the charge or hydrogen bonding capabilities.

 Can a metacentric chromosome be derived from two acrocentric chromosomes?

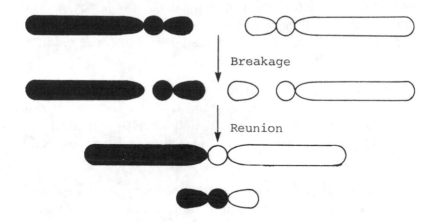

Figure 2.2 — Formation of metacentric chromosomes from reunion of acrocentric types

 Metacentric chromosomes are chromosomes that have their centromeres at or near the middle of their length. Acrocentric chromosomes have their centromeres towards the end of their length. If the acrocentric chromosomes break and rejoin properly, metacentric chromosomes may be formed.

 Can chromosome instability cause cancer?

 There are a number of diseases that result in a high incidence of cancer. Many of these diseases are also associated with an increased frequency of chromosomal instability. This instability causes gaps, breaks, exchanges in, and rearrangement of chromosomal structure. Chromosomal instability may not "cause" cancer but it may create an environment that is highly susceptible to certain forms of cancer.

X*eroderma pigmentosum* is a disease in which the mechanism that repairs ultraviolet induced damage in DNA is defective. In cell culture, clones of affected cells with chromosomal rearrangements have been found. Various skin cancers have been reported in patients with this disorder.

Bloom's syndrome is characterized by dwarfism. Individuals who are homozygous for this recessive trait show a high frequency of spontaneous chromosome breaks in their cells. Individuals with Bloom's syndrome have a high incidence of leukemia and malignant neoplasms.

Individuals who are homozygous or heterozygous for Fanconi's anemia are also cancer-prone. This disorder is characterized by chromosomal aberrations, anatomical defects, and mental retardation.

Victims of these diseases show an instability in their chromosomal structures. They also show a heightened susceptibility to cancer. Since the chromosomes of individuals with these afflictions are easily and effectively disrupted, they must have various defects in the repair pathways that normally protect chromosomes. Although chromosomal instability is not necessarily a cause of cancer, cancer can be one result of chromosomal instability.

Polyploidy and Aneuploidy

 What is the genetic basis of Down's syndrome?

About 10% of the cases of Down's syndrome are caused by a translocation. The translocation chromosome arises as a fusion between chromosomes 14 and 21. A woman who has such a translocation has a normal chromosome 14 and a normal chromosome 21. She also has the translocated chromosome which is designated *t*(14;21). She will be phenotypically normal since she has a full diploid set of chromosomes. However, in meiosis, synaptic pairing is asymmetric and hence the orientation of the spindle can become abnormal. Such a woman may produce eggs that have chromosome 14 but not chromosome 21, 21 but not 14, 21 and $t(14;21)$ or 14 and $t(14;21)$. If an egg with the constitution 21 and $t(14;21)$ is fertilized by a normal sperm containing both chromosomes 14 and 21, Down's syndrome will be the result. The child will have the three copies of chromosome 21 necessary to display Down's syndrome.

Q The chromosomes in a translocation heterozygote consist of two original chromosomes: *ABCDEF* and *GHIJKL*, and two translocated chromosomes: *ABCJKL* and *GHIDEF*. Diagram and explain the viable and lethal chromosome combinations.

A The homologous parts of a chromosome will associate with each other. As shown in Figure 2.3, such an association gives the gene sequence a definite order in a ring-shaped structure. At anaphase I of meiosis the ring is broken and two chromosomes move to each pole of the spindle. If the chromosomes were distributed at random, six different types of gametes would form. The only sets of gametes that would be viable would be the ones that had the complete genetic sequences: *ABCDEF*, *GHIJKL* and *ABCJKL*, *FEDIHG*. The other types of gametes would be unbalanced and hence nonviable since they do not have a complete set of the genetic information. For instance, in the gamete set *ABCDEF*, *ABCJKL*, the sequence *ABC* occurs twice while the sequence *GHI* is missing entirely. The other gamete types are lethal for similar reasons.

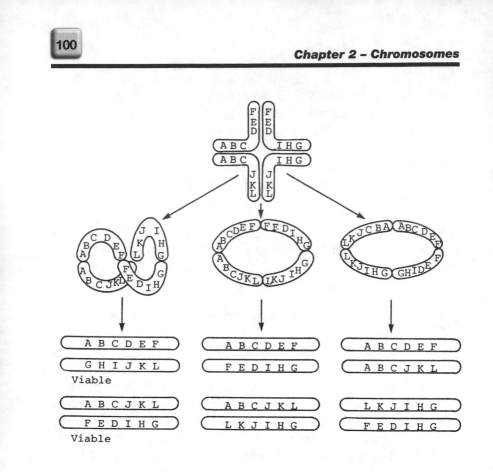

Figure 2.3 — Diagram of viable and lethal chromosome combinations in a translocation heterozygote

 What is the F_1 phenotypic ratio in the jimson weed, *Datura stramonium,* when a purple female (*PPp*) is crossed with a purple male (*PPp*)?

 This problem involves a cross between two individuals that have three alleles for the color of their flowers. Since they have three alleles, they probably have the rest of the chromosomes to go with them. They are, therefore, trisomic. Jimson weed plants that are trisomic in their flower color allele have an extra copy of chromosome 9. In this gene purple is dominant over white. But since these are trisomics, the alleles will not segregate in the usual 3:1 Mendelian ratio, as will be seen.

The female plant produces P, Pp, PP, and p megaspores. The male, on the other hand, only produces functional P and p pollen; pollen with more or less than the normal 12 chromosomes will be nonfunctional.

The cross is shown in the diagram.

By counting the numbers of similar progeny, a genotypic ratio of $4PP$: $4Pp$: $5PPp$: $2Ppp$: $2PPP$: $1pp$ is obtained. The presence of one or more P alleles is expressed phenotypically as purple flowers. White flowers are only expressed in plants homozygous for the recessive p allele. Thus, the phenotypic ratio is 17 purple: 1 white.

PPp ♀ x PPp ♂

gametes: P, P, Pp, Pp, PP, p   P, P, p

Female gametes

		2P	2Pp	PP	P
Male gametes	2P	PP 4	PPp 4	PPP 2	Pp 2
	p	Pp 2	PPp 2	PPp 1	pp 1

Figure 2.4

CHAPTER 3

Mendelian Genetics

By examining large numbers of offspring from crosses between pure breeding strains of peas, Mendel developed mathematical models for predicting the inheritance of traits. To do classical genetics problems, one must understand the concepts that emerged from the work of Mendel and others, and systematically perform the solutions.

Genes exist in like pairs (**homozygous**) or unlike pairs (**heterozygous**), and are located on homologous chromosomes. In heterozygotes, the dominant gene is expressed, while the recessive gene is not.

Each parent randomly contributes one of each kind of chromosome to the **gametes** (eggs or sperm). At fertilization, gametes unite to form a zygote containing two sets of chromosomes, one set from each parent. The probability of any one chromosome going to a gamete is 1/2.

The random movement of chromosomes to either pole is called **independent assortment** and means that chromosomes can be found in different combinations in the gametes.

Genetics problems should be approached methodically:

1. **Key**: Begin each problem with a carefully written key to your symbols. By convention, a gene is designated by a letter, its uppercase is the dominant allele, and its lowercase the recessive. Choose letters with clearly different upper- and lowercases—size alone may not be enough. Always group the same letters (uppercase first) and consistently use the same order throughout the problem. Define genotypes and their phenotypes for more complicated problems.

2. **Cross and gamete determination**: Many problems give information about the parents and ask for the genotypes and/or phenotypes of offspring. Indicate the cross symbolically. For a monohybrid cross (for example, $Aa \times Aa$) you would write two letters, representing the two genes present in each parent.

Determine the types of gametes that each parent can produce. Homozygous parents produce only one type of gamete: AA parents → A gametes; aa parents → a gametes. Heterozygous parents (Aa) produce two types: $1/2$ A gametes and $1/2$ a gametes. Gametes from a monohybrid cross are symbolized by only one letter, those in a dihybrid cross by two different letters, and so on.

Crosses with genes located on separate chromosomes involve independent assortment. To figure out all possible combinations of such genes, use the fork line method. List the alleles for the first chromosome and their probabilities of occurrence. Where two different alleles exist the probability of each will be $1/2$. Each allele on the first chromosome has an equal probability of combining with the alleles on the second chromosome. Therefore, list the alleles present on the second chromosome and their probabilities next to *each* allele on the first chromosome. Read from left to right to determine each type of gamete. Multiply across to determine the probability of occurrence. Gamete determination for $AaBb$ follows:

allele A or a	allele B or b	gametes

$$
\begin{array}{lll}
1/2\ A & \begin{cases} 1/2\ B & \longrightarrow & 1/4\ AB \\ 1/2\ b & \longrightarrow & 1/4\ Ab \end{cases} \\
1/2\ a & \begin{cases} 1/2\ B & \longrightarrow & 1/4\ aB \\ 1/2\ b & \longrightarrow & 1/4\ ab \end{cases}
\end{array}
$$

Gametes can be determined for any number of genes by extending the forks for each new gene and multiplying the probabilities (for homozygous genes, the probability is one). When gametes are correctly determined, they should contain one allele for each gene and, therefore, only one of each kind of letter.

3. **Punnett square:** The union of an egg and sperm is a random event; any sperm may fertilize any egg. Mechanically it may be easier to figure out all possible fertilizations using the Punnett square. List the gametes from one parent along the top and from the other parent along the left side. Fill in the squares horizontally and vertically with symbol, uppercase first. The contents of the squares represent the genotypes of all possible offspring.

step 1

	A	A
A	A	A
a	a	a

$\longrightarrow$

step 2

	A	a
A	AA	Aa
a	Aa	aa

4. **Fork-line method**: The fork-line method can be used instead of the Punnett square, and is recommended when three or more genes are involved. Let's assume that the cross is $AaBb \times Aabb$. Cross each gene separately. List the results of the first cross

($Aa \times Aa$), including probabilities. Then list the results of the second cross ($Bb \times bb$) for each end-product of the first cross (remember independent assortment).

cross $Aa \times Aa$	cross $Bb \times bb$		offspring
1/4 AA	1/2 Bb	$\longrightarrow$	1/8 AABb
	1/2 bb	$\longrightarrow$	1/8 AAbb
1/2 Aa	1/2 Bb	$\longrightarrow$	1/4 AaBb
	1/2 bb	$\longrightarrow$	1/4 Aabb
1/4 aa	1/2 Bb	$\longrightarrow$	1/8 aaBb
	1/2 bb	$\longrightarrow$	1/8 aabb

The probability of the genotypes for the offspring is the product of the probabilities for the genotype for each gene.

5. **Tabulation of results**: List the genotypes indicating their proportions. Referring back to your key, list the phenotypes for each genotype, again indicating proportions. For example,

genotypes — proportion   phenotypes — proportion

AA — 1/4 ⎫
Aa — 2/4 ⎬   dominant — 3/4

aa — 1/4   ⎬   recessive — 1/4

For monohybrid crosses, the genotypic ratio is 1:2:1, and the phenotypic ratio is 3:1. It is possible to determine which gene is dominant by examining F_2 data where there are large enough numbers of offspring; the larger phenotypic class of offspring is the result of at least one dominant gene. Also, when two phenotypically identical parents produce some offspring that are different, the parents' phenotype must be due to a dominant gene.

Note that phenotypically dominant individuals may be homozygous or heterozygous. To determine which, it may be necessary to do a backcross (phenotypically dominant × homozygous recessives). Sometimes biochemical differences can be used for carrier detection.

When you are asked to determine the genotypes of the parents from information given about offspring, a flow diagram or pedigree chart may be helpful. Indicate the known genes symbolically and indicate unknowns with a dash. Using the genotype of the child, try to attribute each gene to the appropriate parent. For example, in the following:

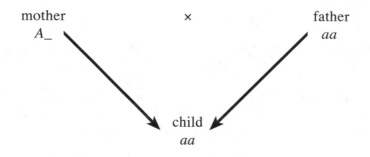

the father contributes one a to the child. Therefore, the other a must have come from the mother. If more than one combination of parents is possible, determine all offspring for each possible cross. Then see which cross best fits the information in the problem.

When the total number of offspring is known, you can determine the expected genotypes and/or phenotypes of offspring by multiplying their probabilities by that total. Actual numbers of offspring may deviate from the expected numbers, since the latter are based upon probabilities.

When determining the frequency of a particular genotype *in a population*, the following equations are used:

p = frequency of dominant gene

q = frequency of recessive gene

$p + q = 1$ frequency of dominant + recessive alleles

Using the Punnett square, we can determine the frequency of the genotypes:

	p	q
p	p^2	pq
q	pq	q^2

$p \times p = p^2$ = frequency of homozygous dominant genotype

$pq + pq = 2pq$ = frequency of heterozygous genotype

$q \times q = q^2$ = frequency of homozygous recessive

$p^2 + 2pq + q^2 = 1$ = frequency of all genotypes

If you are given the frequency of homozygous recessive individuals in a population (q^2), you can take its square root to get the frequency of the recessive allele (q). Subtract the frequency of the recessive allele from one to get the frequency of the dominant allele ($1 - q = p$). Using the values of p and q, calculate the frequencies of homozygous dominant (p^2) and heterozygous individuals ($2pq$).

Problem Solving Examples:

Monohybrid Cross

 Two long-winged flies were mated. The offspring consisted of 77 with long wings and 24 with short wings. Is the short-winged condition dominant or recessive? What are the genotypes of the parents?

Figure 3.1 — Fruit flies (enlarged)

A When we are not told which of the characteristics is dominant and which is recessive, we can deduce it from the ratio of phenotypes in the progeny. We know that 77 flies have long wings and 24 have short wings. This gives us an approximate ratio of 3 long-winged flies to every 1 short-winged fly.

$$\frac{77}{24} \sim \frac{3}{1}$$

As previously noted, the three-to-one ratio signifies that dominant and recessive characteristics are most likely involved. Moreover, because there are three long-winged flies to every short-winged one, it suggests that short-wingedness is the recessive characteristic, and long-wingedness is dominant.

We cannot immediately conclude that both the long-winged parents are homozygous. In fact they are not, because if they were, no short-winged offspring could have resulted in the cross. So the presence of short-winged flies (homozygous recessive) in the progeny suggests that both parents carry the recessive gene and are thus heterozygotes.

Let L be the gene for long wings in flies and l be the gene for short wings in flies. In the cross between two long-winged heterozygous parents:

P	$L\ l$	$\times$	$L\ l$
Gametes	$L;\ l$	$\downarrow$	$L;\ l$
F_1	$1LL :$	$2Ll:$	$1\ l$
	long wing		short wing

The phenotypes of the F_1 show the three-to-one ratio of long-winged flies to short-winged flies, which concurs with the data given. Therefore, the genotypes of the parents are the same, both being heterozygous (Ll).

Q Consider the trait of body color in the flour beetle, *Tribolium castaneum*, to be controlled by a pair of genes exhibiting complete dominance. The pair of contrasting alleles are E for red body which is dominant to e for ebony body color. In a cross between a red-bodied female and an ebony-bodied male, 32 progeny are recovered, of which 18 are red-bodied and 14 are ebony-bodied. What are the genotypes of the parents and progeny?

	male		
		e	*e*
female	*E*	*Ee*	*Ee*
	e	*ee*	*ee*

Figure 3.2

Since the gene for ebony body color is recessive to that for red body color, we can determine the genotypes of both the ebony male parent and ebony progeny to be *ee* homozygotes. The occurrence of ebony progeny dictates that the genotype of the female parent must be *Ee*, since ebony progeny were observed. Similarly, the genotypes of the red progeny must be *Ee* since both parents contribute a gene for body color, *E*, from the female parent and *e*, from the male parent.

The cross can be illustrated by a Punnett square, as shown in Figure 3.2.

Q Consider that in horses a single pair of genes controls gait. Some horses can only exhibit a trotting gait, while others exhibit only a pacing gait. In an attempt to determine the pattern of inheritance displayed by this trait, a horse breeder crossed a stallion (♂) that came from a long line of pacers to several mares (♀) that were trotters. All of the foals were trotters.

Which gait is under the control of the dominant gene?

Using the letters *T* and *t* to represent the dominant and recessive genes, respectively, identify the genotypes of the stallion, the mares and the foals.

A Since all of the foals were trotters, and since both the stallion and the mares came from long lines showing their respective gaits, we can say that the trotting gait is controlled by the dominant gene, T.

Thus, the genotype of the stallion is tt, that of the mares is TT, and the genotypes of the foals is Tt.

Q Given: two strains of snapdragons which differ by a single character: position of the flowers. Strain A has flowers that are positioned axially on the plant stem, while Strain B has terminal flowers. Both strains are considered to be pure breeding for their respective form of the character.

When plants from the two strains are reciprocally crossed (i.e., $A/ \times B$? and $B/ \times A$?), the first progeny generation gives only axially positioned flowers. Second generation progeny exhibited the following:

Phenotype	Number
axial	716
terminal	227

(a) How is this trait inherited?

(b) Using A and a for gene symbols, determine the genotypes for the parent strains, the F_1 generation and F_2 generation progenies.

A (a) Since both strains were pure bred, we can assume that they were homozygous. Therefore, on the basis of the results observed (a 3:1 axial to terminal ratio), the trait appears to be inherited as controlled by a single gene pair. The gene for axially placed flowers is dominant to its counterpart for terminally placed flowers, since only axial flowers were observed in the F_1 progeny. Terminal flowers did not reappear until the F_2 generation.

(b)

Plant	Phenotype	Genotype
Strain *A* parent	axial	*AA*
Strain *B* parent	terminal	*aa*
F_1 progeny	axial	*Aa*
F_2 progeny	axial	*AA* or *Aa*
	terminal	*aa*

Q The ability to roll the tongue into almost a complete circle is conferred by a dominant gene, while its recessive allele fails to confer this ability. A man and his wife can both roll their tongues and are surprised to find that their son cannot. Explain this by showing the genotypes of all three persons.

A Let us represent the dominant allele for the trait of tongue-rolling by *R*, and the recessive allele by *r*. We know that if a gene is dominant for a trait, it will always be expressed if it is present. Since the son cannot roll his tongue, he cannot possess the dominant gene for this trait, and his genotype must be *rr*. This means that each parent must have at least one recessive allele to donate to their son. Also, each parent must have a dominant allele for this trait because they have the ability to roll their tongues. Thus, the genotype of parents for this trait must be *Rr*.

We can illustrate this by looking at the mating of two such parents,

$$P:\quad \text{Father } (Rr) \quad \times \quad \text{Mother } (Rr)$$

$$\downarrow$$

Gametes: *R; r*   *R; r*

F_1		R	r
	R	RR	Rr
	r	Rr	rr

The offspring will be obtained in the following ratio:

F:1/4 *Rr*,   Homozygous dominant; tongue roller.

1/2 *Rr*,   Heterozygous; tongue roller.

1/4 *rr*,   Homozygous recessive; non-tongue roller.

We see then that there is a one-in-four chance that two parents who are heterozygous for a dominant trait will produce offspring without that trait. It is not unlikely, then, that the parents in this problem could have had a son who does not have the ability to roll his tongue.

Dihybrid Cross

Q The checkered pattern of pigeons is controlled by a dominant gene *C;* plain color is determined by the recessive allele *c*. Red color is controlled by a dominant gene *B*, and brown color by the recessive allele *b*. Complete a Punnett square for a dihybrid cross involving a homozygous checkered red bird and a plain brown bird. For this cross, show the expected phenotypes, genotypes, genotypic frequencies and phenotypic ratios for the F_2 generation.

A

P:	$CCBB$	$\times$	$ccbb$
Gametes:	(CB)		(cb)
$F_1 \times F_1$:	$CcBb$	$\times$	$CcBb$

Gametes	(CB)	(Cb)	(cB)	(cb)
(CB)	$CCBB$	$CCBb$	$CcBB$	$CcBb$
(Cb)	$CCBb$	$CCbb$	$CcBb$	$Ccbb$
(cB)	$CcBB$	$CcBb$	$ccBB$	$ccBb$
(cb)	$CcBb$	$Ccbb$	$ccBb$	$ccbb$

This problem involves the Law of Independent Assortment—Mendel's Second Law. The law states that any pair of genes will segregate independently of all other pairs. Because of this, the results of an experiment involving several sets of characters may be obtained by multiplying the proportions expected for each factor when considered individually. The cross would result in the following:

Summary of F_2:

Phenotypes	Genotypes	Genotypic frequency	Phenotypic ratio
checkered red	$CCBB$	1	9
	$CCBb$	2	
	$CcBB$	2	
	$CcBb$	4	

checkered brown	*CCbb*	1	3
	Ccbb	2	
plain red	*ccBB*	1	3
	ccBb	2	
plain brown	*ccbb*	1	1

 In peas, tall (*D*) is dominant to dwarf (*d*) and yellow coty-ledons (*G*) is dominant to green (*g*). If a tall, homozygous, yellow pea plant is crossed with a dwarf, green pea plant, what will be the phenotypic results in the F_1 and F_2?

A Homozygous tall, yellow × Homozygous dwarf, green

$$DDGG \qquad\qquad ddgg$$

F_1 individuals have one gene from each parent in each pair. Hence, *DdGg* are tall and yellow.

The F_2 generation is obtained by mating F_1 individuals.

$DdGg \times DdGg$

This problem can be solved by first determining the results for each individual gene pair.

Dd ×	*Dd*			*Gg* ×	*Gg*	
	D	*d*			*G*	*g*
D	*DD*	*Dd*		*G*	*GG*	*Gg*
d	*Dd*	*dd*		*g*	*Gg*	*gg*

3/4 (*DD* or *Dd*) tall   3/4 (*GG* or *Gg*) yellow

1/4 (*dd*) dwarf   1/4 (*gg*) green

Then apply the rule of probability for independent events. The probability of independent events occurring together is the product of their individual probabilities.

The P of tall and yellow = 3/4 tall × 3/4 yellow = 9/16

The P of tall and green = 3/4 tall × 1/4 green = 3/16

The P of dwarf and yellow = 1/4 dwarf × 3/4 yellow = 3/16

The P of dwarf and green = 1/4 dwarf × 1/4 green = 1/16

These calculations are readily done by multiplying each P for height in the first column times each P for color in the second column.

Q In peas, tall (D) is dominant to dwarf (d) and yellow cotyledons (G) is dominant to green (g). A tall pea plant with yellow cotyledons was crossed with a tall pea plant with green cotyledons. These were the results in the progeny:

6   tall, green
5   tall, yellow
2   dwarf, yellow
2   dwarf, green

What are the genotypes of the parents?

A First, fill in as much of the genotype as possible from the phenotypic description of the parents. If a parent shows a dominant trait, it must possess at least one dominant gene. If it shows a recessive trait, it must be homozygous recessive in the gene pair controlling that trait.

Tall, yellow   ×   Tall, green

$D\_G\_$ D_gg

The rest of the genotype is determined by looking at the progeny. If recessive traits appear in the progeny, both parents must have contributed a recessive gene. Dwarf offspring occur, so both parents must have a *d* gene. Green offspring occur, so the first parent must be heterozygous *Gg*.

$$DdGg \quad \times \quad Ddgg$$

Trihybrid Cross

Q In peas, tall (*D*) is dominant to dwarf (*d*), yellow (*G*) is dominant to green (*g*), and round (*W*) is dominant to wrinkled (*w*). What fraction of the offspring of this cross would be homozygous recessive in all gene pairs?

$$GgDdww \times GgddWw$$

A This problem can be solved using the rule of probability for independent events. The probability of independent events occurring together is the product of their individual probabilities.

First determine the expected frequency of homozygous recessive offspring for each gene pair.

	G	*g*
G	*GG*	*Gg*
g	*Gg*	*gg*

	D	*d*
d	*Dd*	*dd*
d	*Dd*	*dd*

	W	*w*
w	*Ww*	*ww*
w	*Ww*	*ww*

Then, multiply the expected homozygous recessive frequencies together to find the fraction of offspring with all the homozygous recessive gene pairs.

$$1/4 \ gg \times 1/2 \ dd \times 1/2 \ ww = 1/16 \ ggddww$$

Multigene Cross

Q There are two highly inbred strains of laboratory mice whose adult body weights are very different. Assume that the mouse's body weight is under the control of three pairs of contrasting genes: *A* vs. *a*, *B* vs. *b* and *D* vs. *d*. Assume further that each capital letter gene is responsible for contributing 5.0 grams to the total body weight, and that lowercase letters contribute 2.5 grams to total body weight. The average weight of mice in Strain I is 30 grams, while that of Strain II mice is 15 grams.

(a) What are the most likely genotypes of these two strains?

(b) Suppose Strain I and Strain II are crossed. What will be the phenotype of the F_1 progeny?

A (a) Since there are three pairs of genes that control body weight, there will be a total of six genes present. Because the strains are highly inbred, we can assume them to be homozygous. Strain I exhibits a total weight of 30 grams. Since each capital letter gene contributes 5.0 grams, there must be six capital letter genes present. Thus, the genotype of Strain I will be *AA BB DD*. Strain II weighs 15 grams and since each lowercase letter gene contributes 2.5 grams to the body weight, the genotype for this strain will be *aa bb dd*.

(b) Crossing Strains I and II will give an F_1 with a genotype of *Aa Bb Dd*. Thus, with three capital letter genes, each contributing 5.0g, and three lowercase letter genes, each contributing 2.5g, the phenotype of the F_1 will be 22.5g.

Q Assume there is an organism in which there are five contrasting independent gene pairs, *A* vs. *a, B* vs. *b, D* vs. *d, E* vs. *e* and *F* vs. *f*, for which the organism is heterozygous. If the organism were able to undergo self-fertilization,

(a) what is the probability that the first progeny will have a genotype identical to that of the parent?

(b) what proportion of the total progeny will be homozygous?

(c) assuming complete dominance for each gene pair, what proportion of the total progeny will phenotypically exhibit the dominant form for the five characters?

A (a) In a cross between two individuals that are heterozygous for a single pair of genes (e.g., *Aa* × *Aa*), the probability of a progeny being heterozygous is 1/2. Since each of the gene pairs in question are independent, then the probability of the first progeny being identical to that of its parent(s) (i.e., *Aa Bb Dd Ee Ff*) is:

$$P = (1/2)^5 = 1/32.$$

(b)   For a single pair of genes, a cross between two heterozygotes will yield 1/2 of the progeny that are homozygous, eight *AA* or *aa*. Thus, for five independent pairs, the proportion of the total progeny that are homozygous will be

$$(1/2)^5 = 1/32.$$

(c)   A cross between two heterozygotes for a single gene pair with complete dominance will yield 3/4 of the progeny exhibiting the dominant phenotype. Thus, the proportion of the total progeny exhibiting the dominant form for all five characters will be

$$(3/4)^5 = 243/1,024.$$

CHAPTER 4

Sex Determination and

Sex Linkage

Chromosomal and genic controls of sex determination have been observed. The evidence for chromosomal control is the correlation of karyotypes with phenotypic sex. The **heterogametic** sex (containing two kinds of chromosomes) is female in birds, but male in mammals and *Drosophila*. In mammals, maleness is determined by the presence of the Y and femaleness by its absence. For *Drosophila* with a normal chromosome count, the presence of two X's is female-determining, while one X is male-determining. Studies of *Drosophila* with abnormal numbers of chromosomes reveal that the balance of X chromosomes (X) to autosomes (A) is the actual mechanism for sex determination. An X:A ratio that equals 1.0 is female-determining and an X:A ratio that equals 0.5 is male-determining. For organisms in the insect order *Hymenoptera*, haploid organisms are male, and diploid are female. We can use any karyotype, normal or abnormal, to figure out the sex by using the pattern of sex determination for that species.

In mammals, normal males contain one X and normal females two X's. Normal females randomly condense one of their X chromosomes into a Barr body as a means of regulating the level of protein they produce. For abnormal sex karyotypes, all but one X chromosome form Barr bodies. To determine the number of X chromosomes present, count the number of Barr bodies and add one. Also, given a particular karyotype, we can predict the expected number of Barr bodies.

To localize sex determination to a particular portion of a chromosome, chromosomal rearrangements can be studied. Such rearrangements are best visualized by drawing the normal chromosomes showing their long and short arms, then redrawing after breakage and reunion. Rearrangements detected by karyotyping have been correlated with observations of changes in sexual development. When chromosome parts are lost and phenotypic changes observed, the original phenotype can be attributed to the lost region.

Genic sex determination has been observed in a number of organisms. In the case of the parasitic wasp *Habrobracon junglandis,* both genic and chromosomal mechanisms operate in sex determination. The males are haploid and the females are diploid. In addition the s^1 allele causes maleness in both haploid and diploid organisms. By crossing s^1s^3 females with s^1 males, you can demonstrate both types of males among the offspring.

For sex-linked traits—traits that are determined by genes on the sex chromosomes—it is very important to remember that the X and Y chromosomes are not homologous. Genes found on the X are different from those found on the Y. In organisms with homogametic females (one kind of sex chromosome), most sex-linked traits involve X-linkage, since very few genes have been identified on the Y chromosome.

To figure out how the rate of expression of X-linked traits varies in males and females you must understand, first, that human males always express the phenotypes for all X-linked genes, since they only have one X. Thus, recessive as well as dominant genes are always expressed. This condition is termed **Hemizygous**. Second, females have twice as many chances of obtaining an X, since they contain two X chromosomes. Therefore, females express the dominant phenotype whenever there is at least one dominant gene, but need two copies of the recessive gene for expression.

For sex-linkage problems, use the same general approach that you used for autosomal inheritance:

1. **Key**: Since sex-linkage involves a heterogametic and a homogametic sex, it is important to keep track of the sex as well as the trait in sex linkage. Use symbols that include the designation of sex chromosomes, such as X-B, X-b, and Y. For better visualization, you may choose to diagram the sex chromosomes with their genes.

2. **Gamete determination**: Note both X and Y chromosomes.

3. **Punnett square** or **fork line**: When determining the genotypes of the offspring, the X chromosome is listed first, then the Y.

4. **Tabulation of results**: You will understand X-linkage better if you compare it with autosomal inheritance. Remember that autosomal genes in a monohybrid cross always show the dominant phenotype in the F_1 generation and a 3:1 phenotypic ratio in both males and females in the F_2 generation.

For X-linkage, the generations vary depending upon the original cross.

Cross 1 (X-1 linkage)

P_1:	X-B Y	×	X-b X-b
	dominant male	↓	recessive female

F_1:	X-B X-b	×	X-b Y
	dominant females,	↓	recessive males

F_2:	1/4 X-B X-b,	1/4 X-b X-b,	1/4 X-B Y,	1/4 X-b Y
	dominant females	recessive females	dominant males	recessive males

Cross 2 (X-1 linkage)

P_1:	X-b Y	×	X-B X-B
	recessive male		dominant female

F_1:	X-B X-b	×	X-B Y
	dominant females,		dominant males

F_2:1/2 (X-B X-B and X-B X-b),   1/4 X-B Y,   1/4 X-b Y
          dominant females   dominant   recessive
                                                      males   males

X-linkage differs from autosomal inheritance in a number of ways. Recessive individuals appear in the F_1 generation and the F_2 ratio is 1:1:1:1 in cross 1. The only recessive F_2 offspring are males. in cross 2. We can use these patterns to determine whether a trait is dominant or recessive, autosomal or X-linked.

For birds, this pattern is the same except that the sexes are reversed, since the females are heterogametic (or heterozygous).

Traits that are due to Y-linked genes are expressed only in males.

When crosses involve both autosomal and X-linked inheritance, use the Punnett square or fork-line method for problem solving. Note that each gamete contains one sex and one autosomal chromosome.

Pedigree charts are useful for characterizing human families. Males are symbolized as squares and females as circles. A horizontal line between a male and female indicates a mating, and vertical lines to other symbols indicate the offspring. Individuals expressing a trait are denoted by darkened symbols, which may be due to either dominant or recessive genes.

To begin pedigree analysis, draw two blanks to represent the two alleles present in each individual. Fill in as many blanks as possible with information given. For example, a dominant phenotype means at least one dominant gene is present. For X-linkage, the recessive phenotype is represented in a female by two recessive genes and in a male by one recessive and a Y chromosome.

A pedigree chart may tell us whether the trait is dominant or recessive, autosomal or X-linked. A recessive trait is indicated when expressed in the offspring, but not in either parent. Autosomal inheritance is marked by the appearance of the recessive trait in both males and females. X-linkage is characterized by traits expressed predominantly in one sex. Ratios may also be useful if the families are large.

When the inheritance pattern is known, examine each mating in the pedigree in order to determine other genotypes. For each individual whose genotype is known, try to attribute each gene to the correct parent.

Sex-linked traits should be distinguished from sex-influenced and sex-limited traits. Sex-influenced traits are dominant in one sex and recessive in the other. To minimize confusion when problem-solving, the key should include a chart separately listing all genotypes with phenotypes for males and females. When determining the phenotypes of the offspring, refer to the chart.

Sex-limited genes are normally expressed in only one sex. Generally, the expression of these genes is under the influence of sex hormones. Sex-limited genes would be recognized if changes in the hormones of one sex resulted in expression of the phenotype normally characteristic of the other sex.

Problem Solving Examples:

Sex Determination

 Explain the mechanism of the genetic determination of sex in humans.

The sex chromosomes are an exception to the general rule that the members of a pair of chromosomes are identical in size and shape and carry allelic pairs. The sex chromosomes are not homologous chromosomes. In humans, the cells of females contain two identical sex chromosomes, or X chromosomes. In males there is only one X chromosome and a smaller Y chromosome with which the X pairs during meiotic synapsis. Men have 22 pairs of ordinary chromosomes (autosomes), plus one X and one Y chromosome, and women have 22 pairs of autosomes plus two X chromosomes.

Thus, it is the presence of the Y chromosome which determines that an individual will be male. Although the mechanism is quite complex, we know that the presence of the Y chromosome stimulates the gonadal medulla, or sex organ, forming a portion of the egg to develop into male gonads, or sex organs. In the absence of the Y chromosome, and in the presence of two X chromosomes, the medulla develops into female gametes.

In humans, since the male has one X and one Y chromosome, two types of sperm, or male gametes, are produced during spermatogenesis (the process of sperm formation, which includes meiosis). One-half of the sperm population contains an X chromosome and the other half contains a Y chromosome. Each egg, or female gamete, contains a single X chromosome. This is because a female has only X chromosomes, and meiosis produces only gametes with X chromosomes. Fertilization of the X-bearing egg by an X-bearing sperm results in an XX, or female offspring. The fertilization of an X-bearing egg by a Y-bearing sperm results in an XY, or male offspring. Since there are approximately equal numbers of X- and Y-bearing sperm, the numbers of boys and girls born in a population are nearly equal.

 Chromosomal sex in mammals has been shown to be strongly Y chromosome determined. How was this shown to be true?

 From various cytogenetic and chromosomal studies it was found that the presence of a Y chromosome usually determines maleness in mammals. Evidence for this can be seen in the table below. Organisms with an XO set of sex chromosomes were shown to be male in *Drosophila,* but female in mammals. In addition, mammals with an XXY set of chromosomes were shown to be male. The theory was consistently supported by the discovery that males always had at least one Y chromosome while females had at least one X but no Y chromosome.

Individual designation	Sex chromosome constitution	Sex
Normal male	XY	Male
Normal female	XX	Female
Turner female	X	Female
Triplo-X female	XXX	Female
Tetra-X female	XXXX	Female
Penta-X female	XXXXX	Female
Klinefelter males	XXY	Male
	XXXY	Male
	XXXXY	Male
	XXYY	Male
	XXXYY	Male
XYY male	XYY	Male

Table 4.1 — Sex chromosome anomalies and sex determination in humans

How do chromosomal variations influence sex determination in humans?

Chromosomal variations in humans result in intermediate sex individuals. Most of the variants are associated with chromosomal abnormalities involving either an excess or a deficiency of sex chromosomes. With modern techniques it is possible to observe and count human chromosomes accurately. Numbers above and below the usual 46 can be detected. One in every 200 newborns has been shown to have a numerical chromosome irregularity.

The most common sex chromosome anomalies are Turner's syndrome and Klinefelter's syndrome. Turner's syndrome occurs in one out of every 2,000 births. These individuals have 45 chromosomes, and are monosomic for the X chromosome; they are XO. They are short in stature and usually have webbed necks. They are sexually infantile, and often have primary amenorrhea in addition to a failure to develop signs of puberty. Plasma concentrations of follicle stimulating hormone (FSH) and luteinizing hormone (LH) are elevated. The patients lack ovaries, accounting for the failure to develop sexually. Since they have only one X chromosome, buccal smears show no Barr bodies. Therefore, they cannot be distinguished from the cell preparation of a male.

A person with Klinefelter's syndrome has an XXY karyotype and shows male characteristics even though his cells contain Barr bodies. It is sometimes difficult to distinguish these individuals from normal males, although they usually have small testes and are below normal in intelligence. Pubic hair and fat distribution may also follow a female pattern. They are usually sterile.

Other chromosomal variations influencing sex determination have been reported. Males with XXXY, XXYY, and XXXXXY chromosomes are known to exist, as are females with XXX, XXXX, and XXXXX chromosomes. The presence of a Y chromosome is usually linked with "maleness"; the absence of it will lead to an individual with female characteristics.

Q   L. Powers has found that three pairs of genes control the breeding behavior of the guayule plant, *Parthenium argentatum*. The recessive gene *a*, when homozygous, leads to the formation of unreduced eggs; gene *b*, when homozygous, prevents fertilization; and unfertilized eggs will undergo embryogenesis when gene *c* is present in the homozygous form. Because of this, guayule plants of the genotypes *aaBBCC* or *aaBBcc* will reproduce sexually and produce polyploid offspring, while those of genotypes *AABBCC* or *AABBcc* will form diploids through sexual reproduction. *AAbbcc* and *aabbCC* plants are sterile, and *aabbcc* ones are apomictic. If two plants with the genotype *AaBbCc* are crossed, what phenotype ratios can be expected?

A   This problem deals with three segregating gene pairs — a trihybrid cross. The genotype and phenotype ratios from this cross will follow Mendelian principles. One approaches this problem like any other trihybrid cross. Using the forked-lines method, the cross would look like that shown in Figure 4.1.

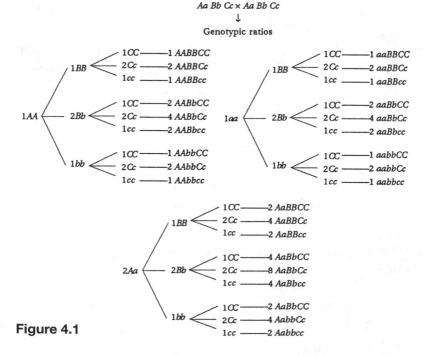

Aa Bb Cc × Aa Bb Cc

↓

Genotypic ratios

Figure 4.1

The phenotypic ratios can be summarized as follows:

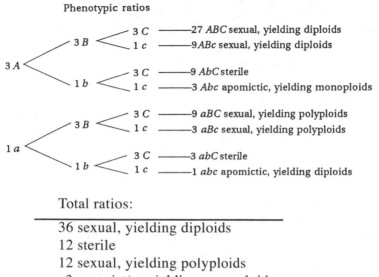

Phenotypic ratios

3 A
- 3 B
  - 3 C —— 27 *ABC* sexual, yielding diploids
  - 1 c —— 9 *ABc* sexual, yielding diploids
- 1 b
  - 3 C —— 9 *AbC* sterile
  - 1 c —— 3 *Abc* apomictic, yielding monoploids

1 a
- 3 B
  - 3 C —— 9 *aBC* sexual, yielding polyploids
  - 1 c —— 3 *aBc* sexual, yielding polyploids
- 1 b
  - 3 C —— 3 *abC* sterile
  - 1 c —— 1 *abc* apomictic, yielding diploids

Total ratios:

36 sexual, yielding diploids
12 sterile
12 sexual, yielding polyploids
3 apomictic, yielding monoploids
1 apomictic, yielding diploids

Q How is sex determination in the parasitic wasp *Habrobracon junglandis* different from the method characteristic of the insect order *Hymenopteca*?

A

P: s^1s^2 ♀ × s^3 ♂

F_1: $s^1 s^3$ ♀ $s^2 s^3$ ♀ s^1 ♂ s^2 ♂

Mate F_1 × F_1 ; for example:

$s^1 s^3$ ♀ × s^1 ♂

F_2: $s^1 s^3$ ♀   ($s^1 s^1$ ♂) s^1 ♂ s^3 ♂

Figure 4.2 — A diploid ♂ homozygous for one of the sex alleles

This wasp is known to produce males by homozygosity as well as parthenogenesis. Parthenogenesis is the development of organisms from unfertilized eggs. In the *Hymenoptera* insect order, these haploid organisms result in male insects. Usually this is the only way for males to develop, but in the parasitic wasp diploid males are also produced by homozygosity at a single gene locus. The diagram shows a cross which results in one of these males.

At least nine sex alleles are known to exist at this gene locus, and the alleles may be represented as s^1, s^2, s^3, ..., s^9. Haploid males carry only one of the alleles at this locus. Diploid females are heterozygous at the locus; examples are the alleles s^1s^2, s^1s^4, or s^3s^4. Any insect that is homozygous for an allele, s^1s^1 or s^8s^8, for example, will develop into a diploid male. Thus, if any allele at this locus, whether present in single or double condition, has no complement with which to interact, it will produce a male insect.

Sex-Linked Traits

Q Hemophilia, a genetic blood disorder, is caused by a recessive sex-linked gene. A phenotypically normal couple had a son with hemophilia. What is the probability that their next child, if a girl, would also have hemophilia?

 The following cross is occurring:

	X^C	Y
X^C	X^CX^C	X^CY
X^c	X^CX^c	X^cY

There is no chance that a daughter will have hemophilia. A daughter would have to be homozygous X^cX^c to have hemophilia. A phenotypically normal father could not pass a gene for hemophilia to any children.

 In humans, the disease known as hemophilia is inherited as an X-linked recessive trait.

Sally and Sam, both of whom are normal, marry, and they have three children: (1) Saul, a hemophiliac, who marries a normal woman and has a daughter, Sarah, who is normal; (2) a normal daughter, Sheryl, who marries a normal man and has a son, Solomon, who is a hemophiliac; and (3) Shirley, also normal, who marries and has six normal sons.

Using the letters *H* and *h* for the normal and hemophilia genes, respectively, and ↗ to represent the Y chromosome, determine the genotypes of Sally, Sam, Saul, Sarah, Sheryl, Solomon, and Shirley.

 Sally must be heterozygous *Hh* since her son Saul is a hemophiliac. Sam's genotype is *H*↗ since he is normal, and Saul's must be *h*↗ since he is a hemophiliac. Sarah, who is normal, receives the hemophilia gene from Saul, and therefore is *Hh*. Since Sheryl has a son who is a hemophiliac she must also be *Hh*. Her son, Solomon, must be *h*↗. Since Shirley had six sons, none of whom was affected, she most likely is homozygous normal, *HH*.

 Red-green color blindness is caused by a recessive sex-linked gene. If a red-green color-blind man marries a woman with normal vision whose father was red-green color blind, what will be the expected phenotypic results in their children?

 Always write out the genotypes of the parents with the sex chromosomes. Remember the Y chromosome carries essentially no genes except those for "maleness."

Red-green
color-blind man   ×   Heterozygous
woman

X^cY X^cX^C

Then solve the problem in the usual way for single gene pairs, but carry along the sex chromosomes.

	X^c	Y
X^C	X^CX^c	X^CY
X^c	X^cX^c	X^cY

Results in progeny:

1/4 female, normal vision

1/4 male, normal vision

1/4 female, color blind

1/4 male, color blind

Q In the fruit fly, *Drosophila melanogaster*, the gene for white eyes is sex-linked recessive, w. Its wild-type allele, w^+, gives dull red eyes. The gene for black body, b, is an autosomal recessive and contrasts its wild-type allele, b^+, which gives a gray body. For a cross between females who are heterozygous for both genes, and white-eyed, black-bodied males, determine the phenotypes of the progeny, and in what proportions they occur.

A We use the Punnett square to solve this problem. First, we determine what gametes are produced by each parent. The genotypes of the parents are *wwbb* for the females and *w⬈bb* for the males.

♀ \ ♂	wb	b
w⁺b⁺	*w⁺wb⁺b* ♀ red, gray	*w⁺⬈ b⁺b* ♂ red, gray
w⁺b	*w⁺wbb* ♀ red, black	*w⁺⬈ bb* ♂ red, black
wb⁺	*wwb⁺b* ♀ white, gray	*w⬈ b⁺b* ♂ white, gray
w b	*wwbb* ♀ white, black	*w⬈ b b* ♂ white, black

Summarizing the progeny, we see that the phenotypic distribution of the progeny is the same for both females and males: 1 red-eyed, gray-bodied: 1 red-eyed, black-bodied: 1 white-eyed, gray-bodied: 1 white-eyed, black-bodied.

Q Consider the gene for vermilion eye color (*v*) in the fruit fly, *Drosophila melanogaster*, to be X-linked and recessive to its wild-type allele (*v⁺*), which produces dull red eye color. The heterogametic sex (XY) in the fruit fly is the male. A female with wild-type eyes is crossed with an unknown male and the following progeny are observed:

Females	Males
64 wild-type	42 wild-type
57 vermilion	59 vermilion

(a) What is the genotype of the female parent?

(b) What is the genotype of the unknown male parent?

 (a) Since the gene for vermilion is recessive and X-linked and, since vermilion-eyed male progeny were observed, the female parent must have been heterozygous, with a genotype of v^+v.

(b)   Since the male can only transmit his X-chromosome to his daughter progeny, and since the female parent was heterozygous, the only way vermilion-eyed female progeny could occur would be for the unknown male to have been $v \nearrow$ in genotype.

Variations of Sex Linkage

Is there a genetic basis for baldness?

Baldness has been explained by several different modes of inheritance by different investigators. Pattern baldness appears to be a sex-influenced trait. Genes governing sex-influenced traits may reside on any of the autosomes or on the homologous portions of the sex chromosomes. The dominant or recessive properties of the alleles of sex-influenced traits is dependent upon the sex of the bearer, due largely to sex hormones.

The gene for pattern baldness is dominant in men, but exhibits recessiveness in women. Indications are that a single pair of autosomal genes control pattern baldness, acting in the following fashion:

Genotype	Male	Female
BB	bald	bald
Bb	bald	nonbald
bb	nonbald	nonbald

The allele seems to exert its effect only in the presence of testosterone.

CHAPTER 5

Mutations and Alleles

Mutations are genic or chromosomal changes that alter the phenotype of the organism. Genic mutations, due to base substitutions, frameshift mutations, or thymine dimers, produce **alleles**—different forms of a particular gene. To understand the chemical basis of mutations, let's look at the chemical nature of the gene. A gene is a sequence of bases in DNA that determines the amino acid sequence of a polypeptide. The sequence of DNA's four bases (adenine, guanine, thymine, and cytosine) is read from one of DNA's two strands. Sixty-one different **triplets** (combinations of three bases) code for twenty amino acids, and three triplets code for termination of the gene message. A mutation or change in any base may change the code to a different amino acid or may cause protein synthesis to end prematurely.

Understanding the bonding between DNA bases is very important in the story of mutation. Normally, the two strands of DNA are held together by hydrogen bonding between bases: adenine with thymine and guanine with cytosine. Thus, the sequence of bases in one strand determines the sequence of bases in the other complementary strand. Other types of base-to-base bonds can occur, producing mutation. Thymine can bond with an adjacent thymine on the same strand. Also, a base on one strand can incorrectly pair with a noncomplementary base on the second strand. If a base change occurs, it can be maintained by normal complementary pairing during DNA replication.

Base substitutions occur by altering the existing base, or by substitution of a new base (base analogues). These changes, whether spontaneous or induced, are important when this new base exists in a form that makes hydrogen bonding to an alternate base possible. When DNA replication occurs, the wrong base can attach, resulting in a different code.

To document the changes that occur during chemical mutagenesis, first diagram the DNA segment in question, then redraw with the appropriate change.

	Base Affected	New Base	Pairs With
Act as Base Analogues:			
5-bromouracil	thymine	5-BU	guanine
2-aminopurine	adenine	2-AP	
Alter Existing Base:			
nitrous acid	adenine	hypoxanthine	cytosine
	cytosine	uracil	adenine
hydroxylamine	cytosine	–OH group	adenine
ethyl ethanesulfonate	guanine	ethyl group added	cytosine or thymine

Redraw the DNA after replication of the aberrant strand, showing the change in pairing of the altered or substituted base. Redraw the DNA after another replication, this time using the new DNA strand as a template.

To understand how a base substitution can alter phenotype, remember that base sequence in DNA determines the amino acid sequence in the polypeptide. Reading frames of triplets code for particular amino acids. A change in a base could create a new triplet coding for a different amino acid or for message termination. The consequences of the change would vary, depending upon how the ability of the polypeptide to function is altered.

The second genic mutation, the frameshift mutation, may occur during DNA repair, as a replication mistake, or due to chemical exposure. To understand the more severe consequences possible, remember that bases are read as triplets during protein synthesis. When one or two bases are added or deleted, the reading frame is altered for all codes following the mutation. If a termination code occurs, a partial polypeptide may form. On the other hand, two frameshift mutations, such as an addition and a deletion, can cancel each other out if located relatively close.

Understanding the severity of genic mutations due to thymine dimers depends upon familiarity with the different types of DNA repair mechanisms. Thymine dimers, typically induced by ultraviolet light, are base pairs between two thymines on the same DNA strand, and cause distortion of the DNA. Enzymes, activated by visible light, split thymine dimers during photoreactivation repair. Excision repair enzymatically recognizes and excises thymine dimers, then fills the gap using the complementary strand as a template. Both repairs restore the DNA. SOS repair, on the other hand, depends upon random filling of gaps created from excision of thymine dimers; it allows cells to replicate even if the genome now contains much erroneous information. Photoreactivation enzymes have been demonstrated in a variety of organisms (bacteriophage, bacteria, protozoa, algae, fungi, yeast, molluscs, arthropods, teleosts, amphibians, birds, marsupials, and placental mammals).

In humans, spontaneous mutation rate is most easily determined for dominant genes with complete penetrance and for sex-linked genes, since males are hemizygous. Recessive mutations may be carried for many generations without being detected. It is estimated that the average person carries 5–8 lethal recessive mutations. Since these are recessive, they are not expressed.

In predicting the consequences of exposure to mutagens, keep in mind that mutation is a random event. The number of mutations induced by any agent is proportional to the length of time exposed to the agent. The random nature of mutation means, however, that there may be variations in numbers of mutations in a small population. Those numbers should average out for a larger population. When samples are taken from the latter, each sample will have about the same number of mutations.

The detection of mutations is based upon finding different structural and/or biochemical phenotypes. Since mutation rates are low, prolific organisms, such as *Drosophila* or bacteria, provide the numbers needed for this type of study.

A particularly useful means of studying mutation is to look for X-linked lethal mutations in irradiated *Drosophila* males. These males are crossed with females whose X chromosomes are marked with two genes: B (Bar eyes) and w^a (apricot eyes). Diagram the crosses for two generations, indicating by color or pattern the X chromosome derived from the irradiated males. When interpreting the results of the F_2 generation, keep in mind that the sex ratio should normally be 1:1. Also, remember that males with X chromosomes carrying lethal mutations will die, because those males are hemizygous.

The Ames test, another way of studying mutation rate, determines the rate of reverse mutation (*his–* ⟶ *his+*) for *Salmonella typhimurium* after exposure to a particular chemical. The mutant strain needs histidine in its diet in order to grow, and, therefore, requires a medium containing histidine. Reverse mutation restores the organism's ability to make its own histidine, and, therefore, allows growth on a minimal medium. After exposure to a chemical, growth on a complete medium reflects the total count of colonies, while growth on a minimal medium reflects the number of reverse mutations. Since bacterial preparations are first diluted before plating (to facilitate growth of isolated colonies), the total colonies on each plate must be divided by their respective dilution factors to obtain the true colony counts. Then,

$$\text{mutation rate} = \frac{\text{number of mutants}}{\text{total number of cells}}$$

In humans, spontaneous mutation rate is most easily determined for dominant genes with complete penetrance and for sex-linked genes, since males are hemizygous. Recessive mutations may be carried for many generations without being detected.

Relative fitness, the relative ability of a parental genotype to contribute to the next generation, can also be used to determine mutation rate, as defined by the following relationship:

$$u = 1/2\ (1 - f\,)x$$

u = mutation rate

f = relative fitness

x = frequency of the genotype in one generation

Relative fitness is determined by the number of offspring produced by affected individuals divided by the number of offspring produced by normal siblings. The frequency of the genotype in one generation is the number of individuals affected divided by the total number of births.

Now let us turn our attention to **alleles**, different forms of the same gene. Since a particular phenotype may be affected by one or more genes, crosses should be done to test for allelism. Diagram one cross showing chromosomes with two different genes (different sites) and diagram a second cross assuming allelism, genes located at the same chromosomal site. Determine the genotype and phenotype of the offspring for each cross.

To understand variation in expression of alleles, you must realize that genes function in different developmental environments with varying genomic backgrounds. Genes may not be expressed at all (variable penetrance) or may be expressed to varying degrees (variable expressivity).

Multiple alleles are due to different mutations in the same gene, resulting in more than two possible phenotypes. In crosses involving multiple alleles, any individual has only two copies of a particular gene, and therefore, at most, two different alleles. Defining an orderly key is most important when working with multiple alleles. Indicate the hierarchy of dominance of alleles when present. Symbolize codominance with the same uppercase letter, using different subscripts for alleles. Also, list all possible genotypes for each phenotype for later reference when determining phenotypes. The problems are then worked as outlined in previous chapters.

Problem Solving Examples:

Mutations

 What is a mutation? List and briefly explain the two major classes of mutations.

DNA sequence integrity is usually maintained from cell division to cell division with a high degree of fidelity. Occasionally, unexpected changes in the DNA sequence occur. These alterations are called mutations. The causes of mutation basically fall into two cases: those resulting from damage to the nucleic acid itself and those resulting from mistakes made by the polymerase during replication. Mutagens act by either directly damaging the DNA or by increasing the frequency at which the polymerase makes errors. Often, mutations must be "fixed" (i.e., made permanent) by inaccurate repair or the passage of one round of replication.

Mutations fall into certain classes. Local mutations involving only one base (or at most a few) are called point mutations. These are usually caused by polymerase errors or direct lesions to the

DNA. Larger mutations such as inversions, translocations, and insertions or deletions involving several base pairs are called chromosome aberrations and are mediated by the host recombination machinery.

 What are the different types of point mutations?

 The major point mutations are base substitutions and small insertions and deletions. Base substitutions fall into two classes: transitions, in which a purine replaces another purine ($A \rightarrow G$ or $G \rightarrow A$ changes) or a pyrimidine replaces another pyrimidine ($T \rightarrow C$ or $C \rightarrow T$), and transversions, in which a purine is changed to pyrimidine or vice versa. Small insertions and deletions usually result from template-polymerase slippages. Insertions or deletions in protein coding regions can be very devastating. If the insertion/deletion is not a multiple of three, a change in the reading frame occurs, resulting in major compositional changes in the expressed protein.

Deletions, Insertions, and Slippage

How does ultraviolet light damage DNA?

Ultraviolet light is a nonionizing form of radiation. It has several effects on DNA, but the major damage of DNA, induced by UV light, is the production of thymine dimers. Thymine dimers are chemical bonds between two adjacent thymine residues as shown in Figure 1. These dimers distort the DNA helix by interrupting the hydrogen bonding between the thymine residues and their complementary adenine residues on the other strand. This interferes with strand replication and leads to mutation or cell death.

Fortunately, thymine dimers are recognized by certain enzymes. The dimers can be made into thymine monomers by photoreactivating enzymes which need a photon of visible light to perform the reaction. Dimers are also recognized by an endonuclease that cuts the helix near the dimer. An exonuclease can then digest the portion of the strand containing the dimer, thus leaving a gap. The gap is filled by a DNA polymerase that uses the complementary strand as a template. Ligase seals the remaining nick. This process is called excision repair.

Most of the dimers induced by UV light are repaired. A faulty excision repair system has been implicated in humans who have xeroderma pigmentosum. Such individuals are homozygous for the mutant allele and are very sensitive to the UV light of sunlight.

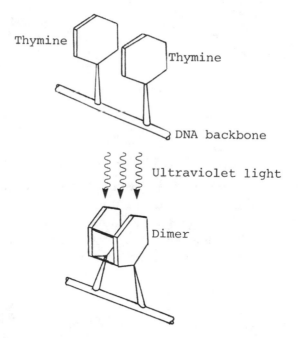

Figure 5.1 — Thymine dimerization between adjacent thymine bases in a single strand of DNA

Is the effect of background radiation in producing spontaneous mutations more significant in humans or in fruit flies?
Why?

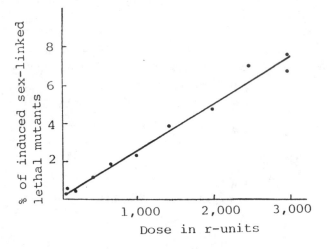

Figure 5.2

 Radiation doses are cumulative with respect to induced mutations. This is because radiation produces ions when it is
absorbed by a cell. Any one of the millions of ions that are produced can be responsible for a genetic change. So the length of
time over which an organism absorbs radiation, even if it is background radiation, will be important in analyzing how effective the
radiation is in inducing mutations.

A fruit fly has an average life span of four weeks. A human has
an average life span of about 75 years. Even if the human being
does not live out his expected life span, he will probably live 20 or
more years. Since the question stated that the radiation was background radiation, the day-by-day exposure of the human and the
fly can be expected to be the same. Thus the human, with his much

longer life span, can be expected to absorb more radiation to induce more mutations than the fruit fly.

Mutation Rate

A dominant trait has a fitness of 0.6. The frequency in a population of this trait is 1 in 8,000. What is the mutation rate?

This problem can be solved by using the equation:

$$b = \frac{2\mu}{1 - w}$$

where b = frequency at equilibrium

μ = mutation rate

w = fitness of a dominant trait.

We are given that the frequency is 1 in 8,000 and the fitness of the trait is 0.6, so:

$$b = \frac{1}{8000}$$

$$w = 0.6$$

$$\mu = ?$$

Plugging these numbers into the formula, we can find the mutation rate, μ:

$$b = \frac{2\mu}{1 - w}$$

$$\frac{1}{8000} = \frac{2\mu}{1 - 0.6}$$

Cross multiplying gives us:

$$16,000 \; \mu = 1 - 0.6$$

$$\mu = 2.5 \times 10^{-5}$$

The frequency of this trait is 2.5 for every 100,000 gametes.

Alleles

 Osteogenesis imperfecta is associated with bone, eye, and ear defects. Some persons show only one defect and others show any combination of the remaining defects. Explain.

 Osteogenesis imperfecta is an autosomal dominant disease that expresses itself in bone abnormality. The bones of affected people are very brittle. The eye and ear defects that are also associated with the allele are expressed in only some of the carriers. The variance in the expressivity is termed just that — expressivity. Expressivity refers to the degree to which the phenotype of an allele is expressed.

The allele for osteogenesis imperfecta also shows pleiotropy. Pleiotropy occurs when a single gene locus has more than one phenotypic effect. Thus, a single dominant allele may express itself in numerous variations.

 What are multiple alleles and how do they originate?

 Multiple alleles are three or more genes that control a single trait. They presumably have arisen from mutations in the same gene of different individuals. Most series of multiple alleles are associated with gradation in a phenotype. For instance, *Drosophila* has a series of mutations in eye color that vary from the wild-type red to the mutant white. Mutants can have apricot, buff, eosin, coral, honey, pearl, or blood colored eyes. In humans, the blood type locus has multiple alleles.

 An actress with O type blood accused a producer with B type blood of being the father of her child in a paternity suit. The child was also O type. What does the blood type suggest about his guilt?

Blood types	Genotypes
A	AA or Aa
B	A^BA^B or A^Ba
AB	A^BA
O	aa

	Actress O type		Producer B type	
Genotype	aa	×	A^BA^B or A^Ba	
	↓ ↓		↓ ↓	
Gametes	a a		A^B a	

	a	a
A^B	A^Ba	A^Ba
a	aa	aa

If the producer were heterozygous for A^B he could father the O type child. This evidence indicates that he could have been the father but does not prove it.

 If a person with O type blood marries a person with AB type blood what will be the expected results in the progeny?

Blood types	Genotypes
A	AA or Aa
B	A^BA^B or A^Ba
AB	AA^B
O	aa

Phenotypes	**O type**		**AB type**
Genotypes	aa	×	AA^B
	↓ ↓		↓ ↓
Types of gametes	a a		A A^B

	a	a
A	Aa	Aa
A^B	A^Ba	A^Ba

1/2 Aa A type

1/2 A^Ba B type

Consider the following three loci in humans, each of which is considered to be a complex locus with multiple alleles: ABO locus (6 alleles), Rh locus (8 alleles), and MN locus (4 alleles). Assuming that each locus is independent of the other two, how many different genotypic combinations can there exist in a given population?

A We first use the formula

$$\frac{x(x+1)}{2}$$

where x = the number of alleles for a given locus to determine the number of possible genotypes for each locus.

For the ABO locus,

$$\frac{6(6+1)}{2} = 21 \text{ genotypes,}$$

the Rh locus gives

$$\frac{8(8+1)}{2} = 36 \text{ genotypes,}$$

and for the MN locus, there are

$$\frac{4(4+1)}{2} = 10 \text{ genotypes.}$$

Since we assume that the three loci are all independent, the total number of different genotypic combinations can be found by multiplying the number of genotypes for each. Thus, 21 × 36 × 10 = 7,560 different genotypic combinations that can exist for these loci.

Q Consider the ABO blood group locus in humans, which has six (6) alleles reported for it, of which three are most prominent, I^A, I^B, and i. The I^A and I^B alleles are both dominant to i and codominant to each other.

A woman of blood group O marries a man who has blood group B. There are four children in the family: a son and daughter of blood group O; a daughter who has A blood type; and a son who has B blood type. One of the children is adopted. Which child is the adopted child?

A Since the mother belongs to blood group O, she and her O daughter and son have the genotype ii. Her husband, who is of blood group B, has to have the genotype $I^B i$, as does the B son. Therefore, the daughter who has blood group A must be the adopted child, for neither parent is a source for allele I^A.

CHAPTER 6

Genetic Interactions

Not all genes follow the classic pattern of simple dominance as indicated by a phenotypic ratio of 3:1 for monohybrid crosses, or 9:3:3:1 for dihybrid crosses. When a different ratio appears, genetic interactions may be the cause.

The first step is to determine the number of genes. Similarity to a 3:1 ratio indicates some variation of a monohybrid cross. An example is **incomplete dominance,** in which heterozygotes have an intermediate phenotype when compared with homozygotes. For incomplete dominance, phenotypic as well as genotypic ratios are 1:2:1.

Another variation on the 3:1 ratio is evident with **lethal genes** — genes that cause the death of the organism before it can reproduce. When the lethal gene is recessive and causes embryonic death, a monohybrid cross gives a ratio of 1 dominant homozygote: 2 heterozygotes. Heterozygotes might be recognized by a characteristic phenotype or by an inability to breed true.

Similarity to a 9:3:3:1 ratio indicates that two independently assorting genes are involved. The following ratios all have 16 as the common denominator: 12:3:1, 9:3:4, 9:6:1, 15:1, 9:7, or 13:3.

Some form of gene interaction causes the modification in ratio. One such interaction is **epistasis:** the ability of one gene to inhibit the expression of another. Different ratios will result depending upon whether the epistatic gene is dominant or recessive. In other interactions, two genes may affect the same characteristic. The effects of the dominant or recessive genes may be cumulative, and may or may not exhibit simple dominance at each gene locus.

In approaching these types of problems, first determine the number of genes involved. For one gene the ratio usually adds to 4, for two genes the ratio adds to 16. Once two genes have been implicated, the type of interaction must be determined. This is best done by trial and error. Carefully construct a key showing allele designations as well as genotypes and phenotypes. Determine genotypes and ratios using the Punnett square or fork-line method. Tabulate genotypes and, referring to your key, translate to phenotypes. If the phenotypic ratio does not match the information given in the problem, redefine the key, and translate the genotypic tabulation using the new key. Eventually you will come to recognize patterns of interaction by their ratios, but you can derive this information rather than depend upon memory.

Polygenic inheritance, the determination of a single phenotypic trait by the additive effect of many genes, can be mechanically cumbersome to solve. Three heterozygous genes produce eight gametes, and a cross of triple heterozygotes requires a Punnett square with 64 boxes. This cumbersome method invites bookkeeplng mistakes. When three or more genes are involved, problems are best worked using the fork-line method (dichotomous branching).

Several methods can be used to determine the number of pairs of polygenes responsible for a particular phenotype. One such method uses the binomial expansion. If the number of phenotypic classes in the F_2 generation is known, the following can be used:

$$\text{\# phenotypes in } F_2 = 2n + 1$$

Solving for n gives the number of pairs of polygenes.

Alternately, the number of pairs of polygenes can be determined if the number of F_2 offspring with the same phenotype as one of the parents is known. Determine the fraction of such F_2 offspring by dividing by the total F_2 offspring. For a monohybrid cross, this fraction should equal 1/4. This class could equal $(1/4)^2$ for a dihybrid cross, $(1/4)^3$ for a trihybrid cross, and $(1/4)^n$ for a cross involving n pairs of polygenes.

A third method for determining the number of polygenes is especially useful when continuous variation in phenotypes occurs rather than distinct phenotypic classes. If the following information is known,

R = difference between mean values of two inbred strains

V_{F_1} = variance of F_1 generation

V_{F_2} = variance of F_2 generation

the number of polygenes (n) can be determined by the formula:

$$n = \frac{1}{8}\left(\frac{R}{V_{F_1} - V_{F2}}\right)$$

The effects of modifier genes can be considered a variation of polygenic inheritance, except that one gene is defined as having a major role in expression of a phenotype. With a well-defined key and the fork-line method, this type of problem becomes easy to solve.

Pleiotropy is the phenomenon of one gene controlling more than one phenotypic effect. The single gene acts via a common developmental pathway to different structural or biochemical events. When the multiple effects are recognized as a syndrome, the inheritance pattern is really very simple since it involves only one gene. Pleiotropy is distinguishable from multiple gene effects in that the characteristics of the syndrome are inherited together and do not segregate.

Phenocopies can also be genetically misleading. These are changes in the organism due to environmental effects rather than to genetics. They may be mistaken for genetic phenomena, especially if there are known genetic controls for the particular phenotype. Only a careful review of family history or crosses involving affected organisms will give evidence of genetics and rule out phenocopies.

Heritability is a measure of the genetic influence on observed variation of a trait in a population. It can range from 0 to 1. To determine the heritability we need the means of the parents, F_1 generation, and population. The formula $H = G/D$ gives heritability (H). Selection gain (G) is the difference between the mean of the F_1 generation and the mean of the population. Selection differential (D) is the difference between the mean of the parents and the mean of the population.

Patterns of inheritance that are not typically Mendelian may be extranuclear inheritance. Where inheritance can be traced to the individual contributing the most cytoplasm, we may be dealing with maternal inheritance. Sometimes nuclear inheritance may be disguised as cytoplasmic, if the nuclear control results in a cytoplasmic product that influences the development of the next generation. When this happens, the next generation may show nuclear inheritance ratios, as is found in snail swirls.

Problem Solving Examples:

Codominance

 In snapdragons, plants homozygous for red have red flowers; those homozygous for white have white flowers, and those which are heterozygous have pink. If a pink flowered snapdragon is crossed with a white flowered plant, what will be the expected phenotypic results in the progeny?

This is a case of incomplete dominance. Red (*R*), White (*R´*), heterozygous pink individuals are *RR´*.

	Pink flowered		White flowered
Genotypes	*RR´*	×	*R´R´*

Types of gametes: *R*   *R´*   *R´*   *R´*

	R	*R´*
R´	*RR´*	*R´R´*
R´	*RR´*	*R´R´*

Phenotypic results: 1/2 *R´R* pink

1/2 *R´R´* white

The color and shape of radishes are controlled by two pairs of alleles that sort independently and show no dominance. Round shape is controlled by the *L´* allele; length is controlled by the *L* allele. Heterozygous radishes (*LL´*) are oval. The *R* allele produces red radishes and the *R´* allele produces white. Purple flowers are produced by RR' heterozygous plants. Using the checkerboard method, diagram a cross between red long ($RRLL$) and white round ($R'R'L'L'$) radishes to get the F_1 phenotypic and genotypic results. Then using a Punnett square, show a cross between F_1 progeny to obtain F_2. Summarize the F_2 phenotypic and genotypic results.

P:	$RRLL$	×	$R'R'L'L'$
Gametes:	RL	×	$R'L'$
F_1:		$RR'LL'$	

All of the F_1 progeny are purple and oval.

F_1 cross: $R'RLL' \times RR'LL'$

Gametes	RL	RL'	$R'L$	$R'L'$
RL	$RRLL$	$RRLL'$	$RR'LL$	$RR'LL'$
RL'	$RRLL'$	$RRL'L'$	$RR'LL'$	$RR'L'L'$
$R'L$	$RR'LL$	$RR'LL'$	$R'R'LL$	$R'R'LL'$
$R'L'$	$RR'LL'$	$RR'L'L'$	$R'R'LL'$	$R'R'L'L'$

F_2 results:

Phenotypes	Genotypes	Genotypic ratio	Phenotypic ratio
red, long	$RRLL$	1	1
red, oval	$RRLL'$	2	2
red, round	$RRL'L'$	1	1
purple, long	$RR'LL$	2	2
purple, oval	$RR'LL'$	4	4
purple, round	$RR'L'L'$	2	2
white, long	$R'R'LL$	1	1
white, oval	$R'R'LL'$	2	2
white, round	$R'R'L'L'$	1	1

Because dominance is not expressed, the genotypic and pheno-typic ratios are identical.

 What is epistasis? Distinguish between the terms *epistasis* and *dominance*.

Genotypes	A_B_	A_bb	aaB_	aabb
Classical ratio	9	3	3	1
Dominant epistasis	12		3	1
Recessive epistasis	9	3	4	
Duplicate genes with cumulative effect	9	6		1
Duplicate dominant genes	15			1
Duplicate recessive genes	9	7		
Dominant and recessive interaction	13		3	

Several genes are usually required to specify the enzymes involved in metabolic pathways leading to phenotypic expression. Each step in the pathway is catalyzed by different enzymes specified by different wild-type genes. Genetic interaction occurs whenever two or more genes specify enzymes involved in a common pathway. If any one of the genes is mutant, the pathway is blocked and genes after it in the pathway cannot have any phenotypic effect. We normally say that the mutant gene is *epistatic* to the suppressed gene.

When epistasis is involved in a dihybrid cross, the classical 9:3:3:1 ratio is modified into ratios which are various combinations of the classical groupings, resulting in less than four phenotypes. Six types of epistatic ratios are commonly recognized. A summary of them appears in the table.

Epistasis can involve any of these ratios.

Dominance involves *intra-allelic* gene suppression, where masking effects are seen between alleles at the same locus. Epistasis involves *inter-allelic* gene suppression between genes of different loci.

Q In snapdragons, the genes *R* and *T* are necessary for tall plants. In the absence of either or both genes, a plant will be dwarf. For the following crosses, determine the phenotypic ratio for the progeny:

(a) *Rrtt* × *RrTt* ♂

(b) *RrTt* × *rrtt* ♂

A (a) We use the Punnett square to get:

♀＼♂	*RT*	*Rt*	*rT*	*rt*
Rt	*RRTt* tall	*RRtt* dwarf	*RrTt* tall	*Rrtt* dwarf
rt	*RrTt* tall	*Rrtt* dwarf	*rrTt* dwarf	*rrtt* dwarf

Thus, the phenotypic ratio will be 5 dwarf: 3 tall.

(b)   The Punnett square constructed for this cross will yield:

♀ ♂	rt	
RT	*RrTt*	tall
Rt	*Rrtt*	dwarf
rT	*rrTt*	dwarf
rt	*rrtt*	dwarf

Thus, the phenotypic ratio will be 3 dwarf : 1 tall.

Polygenic Inheritance

 Two 30" plants are crossed, resulting in progeny of the following ratio: one 22", eight 24", twenty-eight 26", fifty-six 28", seventy 30", fifty-six 32", twenty-eight 34", eight 36", and one 38". Starting with *A* and going through the alphabet to represent different alleles, what are the most probable genotypes of the parents?

The total number of phenotypic classes in the F_2 generation is given by the formula:

# of phenotypes = $2n + 1$,

where *n* = the number of pairs of polygenes.

There are nine phenotypic classes, so:

$2n + 1 = 9$

$n = {}^8/_2 = 4$ = total number of pairs of polygenes.

We can symbolize the genes for height with the capital letters *A* through *D* and their corresponding alleles with the lowercase letters *a* through *d*. Because the height of both parent plants is 30" their genotypes must be identical. The only genotypes that could have produced the phenotypes in the same ratio as resulted are *AaBbCcDd* × *AaBbCcDd*. If you are not convinced of this, work this cross out with a Punnett square or the forked-line method to prove it.

Q Two races of corn averaging 48 and 72 inches in height are crossed. The height of the F_1 generation does not vary very much, averaging 60 inches. When 500 of these plants were classified, two were 48 inches, and two were 72 inches, the rest falling between these in height. What is the number of polygenes involved, and how many inches does each contribute?

A The fraction of the F_2 generation, like a single parent, is given by the formula $(1/4)^n$ where n = the number of pairs of polygenes.

In the F_2 generation, two out of 500 are 48" in height and two are 72". Therefore, the fraction of F_2 like a single parent

$$= \frac{2}{500} = \frac{1}{250}$$

Considering the formula $(1/4)^n$ we see that the series goes 1/4 when $n = 1$, 1/16 when $n = 2$, 1/64 when $n = 3$, etc. 1/250 is closest to 1/256, when $n = 4$. Therefore, we must be dealing with four pairs of alleles, or eight polygenes.

The total height difference between the shortest and tallest plants in the F_2 is 72 – 48 = 24. Dividing 24 into the total number of polygenes, 8, we can find how much height each polygene contributes to the plant:

$$\frac{24"}{8} = 3"$$

Q Although it is possible to categorize eye color in humans into blue or brown phenotypic classes, there are clearly many variations in hue within the two classes. What type of inheritance mechanism may be working to produce eye color?

A Human eye color can be regarded as controlled by one principal gene that is influenced by other genes called modifiers. The main gene has two alleles—dominant *B* for brown eyes and recessive *b* for blue eyes. Blue eyes (*b/b*) owe their color to the scattering of white light by the almost colorless cells of the outer iris. This affect is greatest in the shorter wavelengths, the blues, thus giving the iris its blue appearance. Brown-eyed people (*B/B*) or (*B/b*) have melanin on the front layer of the iris and, thus, do not scatter as much light through their irises. One gene controls whether the eye will be blue or brown, but many modifier genes produce variations on the shade. Some affect the amount of pigment in the iris, some the tone of the pigment, and some the distribution of the pigment. These modifiers can lead to variations on the blue tone, as in the case of gray or green eyes; or, they can change brown pigment, leading to brown variations such as black. Two blue-eyed people can occasionally have a brown-eyed child because one of them has a lack of pigmentation due to modifier genes and actually has the *B/b* genotype.

Q Plants with red flowers are often observed to also have red stems while the white flowered varieties of the same species have green stems. What is this phenomenon, in which a single pair of alleles has more than one phenotypic affect? What are some other examples?

A This phenomenon is called pleiotropism. The condition in which a single gene has more than one effect on an individual is called pleiotropy. Although in the given example the gene pair only affects two different characteristics, it can affect many more as in sickle cell anemia.

In *Aquilegia vulgaris* there is a gene that elicits red flowers, increases the length of the stems, confers darkness to the endosperm, and increases seed weight. A gene for white eyes in fruit flies also affects the structure and color of internal organs, causes reduced fertility, and reduces longevity.

An example of a pleiotropic affect in man is Marfan's syndrome. One gene causes both an abnormality of the eye lens and extremely long fingers.

Environmental Interaction

 What is a phenocopy? How can one differentiate between a phenocopy and a mutation?

A phenotype produced by the environment that simulates the effects of a known mutation is called a phenocopy. It is thought that environmental agents influence the same chemical reactions as mutations do and produce effects similar to the ones produced by mutations. Unlike mutations, phenocopies cannot be inherited.

One would test to differentiate between a mutation and a phenocopy by making specific crosses in order to see whether the phenotypic change is transmitted to progeny.

By injecting boric acid into chicken eggs at a particular stage of development, chickens with short legs are produced resembling the genetic "creeper" trait. A chick with shortened legs resembling the "creeper" effect can be tested to see if it was caused by a mutation or the teratogenic agent boric acid by crossing it with a normal chicken. If the abnormality was produced by the boric acid, there should not be any "creepers" in the progeny. Presumably, the teratogenic agent interferes with gene function during development but it does not permanently change genes.

CHAPTER 7

Linkage, Recombination, and Mapping

Linkage is the inheritance of genes on the same chromosome as a group. The distance between two genes on the same chromosome allows for crossing over between homologous chromosomes, and, therefore, recombination of the genes. The frequency of recombination can be used to map genes on the chromosome.

We can distinguish between linkage and independent assortment by examining the ratio of offspring in a cross between heterozygous (*AaBb*) and homozygous recessive (*aabb*) individuals. When independent assortment occurs, the heterozygote produces four types of gametes in equal proportions (*AB, Ab, aB, ab*) and, therefore, four types of offspring in equal proportions (*AaBb, Aabb, aaBb, aabb*).

For linkage, most offspring will be similar to the parents (parental types), with the recombinant class occurring in lesser numbers. The frequency of the various classes tell us whether the genes are linked or located on different chromosomes. If the linked genes are very far apart, the recombination frequency may be so great that the genes may appear to independently assort. In that case, linkage has to be tested with other genes located closer to the two genes in question.

The **recombination frequency** is defined by the formula

$$\text{recombination frequency} = \frac{\text{\# recombinants}}{\text{total number of progeny}}$$

The distance between genes in map units can be determined by multiplying the recombination frequency by 100.

Three point crosses (involving three genes) were devised to collect as much data as possible in one experiment. However, mapping problems are most easily handled by analyzing two genes at a time. Autosomal linkage problems require that each gene be heterozygous in one individual and homozygous recessive in the other. For X-linkage, the heterozygous females are crossed with hemizygous males for the recessive gene. In either autosomal or X-linked inheritance, eight phenotypic classes are produced.

When preparing the key, the eight phenotypic classes should be listed with their respective symbols, rather than listing alleles separately. This will make reading of the key easier when translating symbols at a later time.

Organize the results of the cross by listing the symbols for the phenotypic classes with their respective numbers. Identify each class type:

Parental classes: The two largest classes can be identified as the parental types.

Double crossovers: The two rarest classes are due to double crossovers. In cases where double crossovers are inhibited, these two classes may not be present, resulting in six instead of the expected eight different classes. For ease of solution you may want to list the double crossover phenotypes anyway, and indicate that the frequency is zero.

Single crossovers: The last four classes can be recognized as two different types of crossovers. Two classes are due to a single crossover between the first two genes, and are recognized by the reciprocal nature of the phenotype and similarity in numbers. The other two classes are due to a single crossover between the second two genes and are, likewise, recognized by their reciprocal nature as well as by their number similarity.

The order of the genes can be determined by comparing the parental classes with double crossover classes. How would two crossovers produce the genotypes listed for double crossovers? Try the three orders possible (for example, *abc, bac,* or *acb*) and see which order gives the genotypes observed for the double crossover classes.

Now let's work with the first two genes and ignore the third gene. Add the four classes that show recombination between these genes, divide by the total offspring, and multiply by 100 to obtain the map units between the first two genes. Repeat this process two more times: for the second and third genes, then for the first and third genes.

If the gene order was not previously determined, it can be now. Two distances should approximately equal the third. The longest distance reflects recombination between the outermost genes. The third gene therefore, is in-between.

If the two distances added together give a longer distance than that observed, double crossovers were inhibited. The expected double crossover frequency can be calculated by multiplying the recombination frequencies for the two single crossovers.

A measure of the inhibition of one crossover by another is called interference. This is expressed as

$$\text{interference} = 1 - \text{coincidence}$$

where

$$\text{coincidence} = \frac{\text{observed double crossover frequency}}{\text{expected double crossover frequency}}$$

When there is no inhibition of crossover, observed and expected double crossover frequencies should be equal; in this case coincidence equals 1 and interference equals 0. As inhibition increases, interference also increases.

It is possible to use the expected double crossovers, the coefficient of coincidence, and map distances to predict the number and types of offspring that should be observed for a particular cross. The expected double crossovers equal the distance between the first and second genes multiplied by the distance between the second and third genes multiplied by the total number of offspring. The number of observed double crossovers equals their frequency (as determined from the coefficient of coincidence) multiplied by the total offspring expected. To find the number of organisms due to a single crossover between the first two genes, perform the following:

$$\frac{\text{map distance between first two genes}}{\text{total offspring}} = \text{double crossover frequency}$$

Repeat for single crossovers between the second two genes. Subtract all crossovers from the total to find the number of parental types.

In the case of *Neurospora*, the ascospore order can help us map genes on a chromosome. Since meiotic products remain in order in the ascospore, crossing over will be reflected in a disruption of that order. If recombination occurs between the centromere and the gene being mapped, there will be a 2:2:2:2 order. The frequency of recombinants divided by the total gives the map distance to the centromere.

For human gene mapping, pedigree analysis can be used when the matings are between heterozygotes and recessive homozygotes (or hemizygous males). Other mapping techniques depend upon knowledge of modern molecular techniques. **Somatic cell hybridization**—the fusion of human and mouse cells—results in the loss of most human chromosomes during their slower mitotic division. Correlation of the remaining human chromosomes or fragments (as determined by karyotyping) with human proteins present maps the genes responsible. Recombinant DNA hybridization probes are created from cloned genes. Hybridization with fragments of human chromosomes indicates location.

As mentioned before, the recombination frequency can be used as a way of determining map distance. To determine whether frequency correlates with actual distance, we have to look at the experimental results. Genes have been mapped on *Drosophila* chromosomes using the difference in appearance of the genes in different allelic form. These cytologically-determined distances are not the same as the distances determined by recombination frequencies. The differences have been attributed to variations in the crossover frequency along the chromosome length.

Problem Solving Examples:

Linkage and Recombination

Q In a given organism, two pairs of contrasting genes are under investigation: *A* vs. *a* and *B* vs. *b*. An F_1 individual resulting from a cross between two homozygous strains was testcrossed, and the following testcross progeny were recovered:

Phenotype	Number
A B	621
A b	87
a B	92
a b	610

(a) Are these two genes linked or independent?

(b) If linked, what is the amount of recombination that has occurred between them?

(c) What are the genotypes of the original homozygous strains?

A (a) The determination of linkage or independence can be made very readily. The expected distribution of testcross progeny for independent gene pairs is a 1:1:1:1 ratio for each of the phenotypic classes. A glance at the data reveals that they are not in a 1:1:1:1: ratio; therefore, the two genes must be linked together in the same chromosomal unit.

(b)   Having determined that the genes are linked, we can find the amount of recombination that has occurred by using the formula

$$\% \text{ recombination} = \frac{\text{total number of recombinant progeny}}{\text{total number of textcross progeny}} \times 100$$

The recombinant progeny are represented by the phenotypic classes that have the lesser numbers. Looking at our data, we see that the classes *Ab* and *aB* have the lowest number of individuals, and are therefore the recombinant classes.

$$\text{Thus, } \% \text{ recombination} = \frac{179}{1,410} \times 100 = 12.7\%.$$

(c) The genotypes of the original homozygous strains can be determined by finding the parental progeny which are represented by the phenotypic classes that have the larger numbers. These are the classes *AB* and *ab*, since these represent the original combinations of the two genes, the genotypes of the parent stocks were

$$\frac{A \quad B}{A \quad B} \quad \frac{a \quad b}{a \quad b}.$$

Two-Point Cross

Q In fruit flies, black body color (b) is recessive to the normal wild-type body color (b^+). Cinnabar eye (cn) is recessive to the normal wild-type eye color (cn^+). A homozygous wild-type fly was mated to a fly with black body and cinnabar eyes. The resulting heterozygous F_1 fly was mated to a fly with black body and cinnabar eyes. These were the results in the offspring:

90 wild-type

92 black body and cinnabar eyes

9 black body and wild-type eyes

9 wild-type body and cinnabar eyes

What is the map distance between the gene for black body and the gene for cinnabar eyes?

A If genes are on the same chromosome they are said to be linked because they will tend to be inherited together. If linkage is involved, genes will tend to remain in the original parental combinations. Combinations unlike either of the original parents will tend to be much less frequent than would be expected from independent assortment. In this example the categories containing only nine individuals represent individuals unlike either of the original parents. These types resulted from crossing over or exchange of chromatid segments between the two gene loci. The amount of crossing over is proportional to the distance between genes. The map distance is determined by dividing the number of crossover types by the total number of offspring.

$$\frac{18}{200} = 0.09$$

This is converted to percent by multiplying by 100; moving the decimal point two places to the right. One percent of crossing over equals one map unit. These two gene loci are therefore nine map units apart.

 In *Drosophila,* the genes black (*b*) and vestigial (*vg*) are 20 chromosome map units apart. In an original cross between black, normal-winged females and normal-bodied, vestigial males, F_1 flies were recovered. If the F_1 flies are intercrossed, predict the phenotypic classes and the number of flies in each, if 1,500 F_2 progeny were classified.

A Since we know the distance between two loci, we can predict the frequency of both the recombinant and the parental gametes produced. From this we can predict the progeny genotypes and phenotypes, including their respective frequencies in the following manner:

The F_1 females will produce the parental gametes *b*+ and +*vg* at a frequency of 0.4 each, and will produce the recombinant gametes *b vg* and + + at a frequency of 0.1 each. Since there is little or no recombination in the male of *Drosophila,* the F_1 males will only produce the parental gametes at a frequency of 0.5 each.

We now use the Punnett square to complete our prediction.

♀ \ ♂	*b* +	+ *vg*
0.4 *b* +	$\dfrac{b+}{b+}$ 0.20	$\dfrac{b+}{+vg}$ 0.20
0.4 + *vg*	$\dfrac{b+}{+vg}$ 0.20	$\dfrac{+vg}{+vg}$ 0.20
0.1 + +	$\dfrac{b+}{++}$ 0.05	$\dfrac{+vg}{++}$ 0.05
0.1 *b vg*	$\dfrac{b+}{b\,vg}$	$\dfrac{b\,vg}{+\,vg}$ 0.05

Summarizing the phenotypes that will result from this cross, we have

    + +   0.50

    b +   0.25

    + *vg*   0.25

    b vg 0

Thus, we see that phenotypic distribution will be 2:1:1:0 because of the failure to observe recombination in the male. We can now convert these frequencies into numbers simply by multiplying them by the total number of flies recovered.

    + +   (0.50) × 1,500   =   750

    b +   (0.25) × 1,500   =   375

    + *vg*   (0.25) × 1,500   =   375

    b vg   =   0

    Total   1,500

Q The gene *r*, for rosy eyes, is 12 map units away from the gene *k*, for kidney-shaped eyes. Both of these genes are recessive to their wild-type alleles. If a heterozygous wild-type fly, resulting from a cross between a homozygous wild-type fly and a fly with rosy, kidney-shaped eyes, is crossed to a fly with rosy, kidney-shaped eyes, what will be the types of gametes and the frequencies of each?

 A The cross is shown in Figure 7.1.

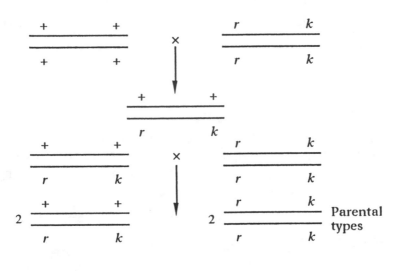

Figure 7.1

Since the distance between the two loci is 12 map units, 12 percent of the progeny will undergo recombination to produce additional types of gametes.

Since crossing over is a reciprocal exchange there should be two crossover types of equal frequency for both parental and recombinant classes.

$$\text{Recombinants } 12\% = \frac{12}{100} = 0.12$$

$$\frac{0.12}{2} = 0.06 \text{ for each type of recombinant}$$

The remaining 88 percent are parental types.

$$88\% = 0.88$$

$$\frac{0.88}{2} = 0.44 \text{ for each type of parental}$$

Thus, our gametes will be as follows:

0.44 + +
0.44 *r k* } Parental types

0.06 *r* +
0.06 + *k* } Recombinant types

Mapping

Q The actual physical distances between linked genes bear no direct relationship to the map distances calculated on the basis of crossover percentages. Explain.

A In certain organisms, such as *Drosophila*, the actual physical locations of genes can be observed. The chromosomes of the salivary gland cells in these insects have been found to duplicate themselves repeatedly without separating, giving rise to giant bundled chromosomes, called polytene chromosomes. Such chromosomes show extreme magnification of any differences in density along their length, producing light and dark regions known as banding patterns. Each band on the chromosome has been shown by experiment to correspond to a single gene on the same chromosome. The physical location of genes determined by banding patterns gives rise to a physical map, giving absolute distances between genes on a chromosome.

Since crossover percentage is theoretically directly proportional to the physical distance separating linked genes, we would expect a direct correspondence between physical distance and map distance. This, however, is not necessarily so. An important reason for this is the fact that the frequency of crossing over is not the same for all regions of the chromosome. Chromosome sections near the centromere regions and elsewhere have been found to cross over with less frequency than other parts near the free end of the chromosome.

In addition, mapping units determined from crossover percentages can be deceiving. Due to double crossing over (which results in a parental type), the actual amount of crossover may be greater than that indicated by recombinant type percentages. However, crossover percentages are nevertheless invaluable because the linear order of the genes obtained is identical to that determined by physical mapping.

Population Genetics

The **Hardy-Weinberg Law** states that gene frequencies and genotype frequencies remain constant in succeeding generations in a population at equilibrium. For allele frequencies, the sum of the allele frequencies equals 1 (one). Thus, for two alleles,

$$p + q = 1.$$

For genotype frequencies,

$$(p + q)^2 = 1 \text{ or } p^2 + 2pq + q^2 = 1.$$

A population at equilibrium satisfies the following assumptions:

1. Large population (no genetic drift or sampling error)

2. Random mating

3. No natural selection (equal viability and fertility of offspring)

4. No mutation

5. No migration

If any of these assumptions is not met, the population is not at equilibrium and is, therefore, changing from generation to generation.

There are a number of methods for determining whether a natural population is at equilibrium. One method is to determine allele and genotype frequencies for more than one generation. If the frequencies change, the population is not at equilibrium.

Another method can be used when the heterozygotes in the population can be identified. Use the frequency of recessive homozygotes (q^2) to determine q. Determine p by the formula

$$1 - p = q.$$

Determine the genotype frequencies of dominant homozygotes (p^2) and heterozygotes ($2pq$), and compare with observed frequencies. If observed and expected frequencies for dominant homozygotes and heterozygotes are the same, the population is at equilibrium for that gene. If the population is not at equilibrium, then one or more of the assumptions does not hold.

Hardy-Weinberg is also useful for studying multiple allele systems. For three alleles, the allele frequencies are

$$p + q + r = 1$$

and the genotype frequencies are

$$(p + q + r)^2 = 1 \text{ or } p^2 + 2pq + q^2 + 2pr + r^2 + 2qr.$$

You can either solve for genotype frequencies when allele frequencies are known, or solve for gene frequencies when phenotype and genotype frequencies are known.

When setting up a Hardy-Weinberg problem involving three alleles, list the equations for allele frequencies and for genotype frequencies. List as many terms for each equation as are defined in the problem. Define the phenotype for each genotype, and where possible indicate phenotype frequencies (you may be able to generate other equations for phenotypes). Solve any equations where only one unknown exists. Use the value of that unknown to solve other equations.

Hardy-Weinberg can be used to predict the results of specific matings. Use the Punnett square to determine the probability of a particular genotype or phenotype appearing among the offspring of the mating defined in the problem. For example, the probability of phenotypically dominant offspring being produced by parents heterozygous for one gene is 3/4. Next, determine the frequencies of the parents in the population. Multiply the frequency of each parent in the population to obtain the probability of a mating between individuals with those genotypes (remember that the probability of two events occurring simultaneously is the probability of the first event multiplied by the probability of the second event).

Finally, multiply the probability of the specific mating by the probability of the specific genotype or phenotype to get the probability of particular offspring appearing for a particular cross. If you want to know what proportion of the next generation will occur because of this particular cross, you must also determine all ways that these particular offspring will appear and divide that number into the probability previously determined.

When a population changes over time, you can calculate the changes by adding or subtracting the change from the original Hardy-Weinberg values. The reasons for change may include migration, net mutation (forward as opposed to back mutation), matings (self-fertilization, between populations), and variability of viability of offspring (lethal genotypes, heterosis). Use the Hardy-Weinberg equations and modify the values for the next generation based upon frequency changes given or calculated from information in the problem. For example, if a particular genotype is lethal, list all matings possible and the frequency of offspring from each mating. To determine the frequency of each type in the next generation, add the frequencies for each type of offspring and divide by the frequency of viable offspring produced.

Hardy-Weinberg can also be used for X-linked genes. Since males are hemizygous, $p + q = 1$ defines the male genotype frequencies as well as the allele frequencies. The formula

$$p^2 + 2pq + q^2 = 1$$

defines the genotype frequencies for the female.

Twin studies are useful in evaluating environmental, as opposed to genetic, influences. Monozygotic twins develop from the same fertilized egg and are, therefore, genetically identical (except for somatic mutations). Dizygotic twins develop from two fertilized eggs and are genetically as similar as siblings born at different times. The assumption is that the members of both twin types exist in very similar environments.

If a trait is genetic in nature, it is expected that the monozygotic twins will be more like each other than dizygotic twins. A method for comparing similarities among twin pairs is concordance. The frequency of concordance

$$= \frac{\text{number of pairs where both show trait}}{\text{number of pairs where at least one shows trait}}$$

When a genetic trait has variable penetrance, the concordance figures will be altered. To determine the frequency of concordant monozygotic twin pairs expected, square the frequency of penetrance.

For pedigree analysis, charts are drawn to symbolize a trait in a family. Squares represent males, circles females, and filled-in symbols represent individuals exhibiting the trait. Horizontal lines between a male and female represent a mating, and vertical lines lead to the offspring. Roman numerals designate generation number and Arabic numbers indicate the age order within a generation.

When analyzing a pedigree, fill in the known phenotypes and genotypes for each individual. If you are asked to determine whether the trait is dominant or recessive, look for a mating that produces offspring that are different from the parents. The offspring would be recessive homozygotes. When distinguishing between autosomal and X-linked inheritance, expect an equal distribution of the trait among both sexes in the former. For X-linkage, a heterozygous female mating with a dominant male is especially instructive, since the recessive phenotype will only show among some male offspring.

To find the probability that a person in the pedigree mated to a carrier from the general population will produce a child with a particular trait, we determine the probability that the person carries the trait, the probability that the person's gametes carry the gene for the trait, and the frequency of carriers in the population. These three probabilities are then multiplied to get the probability that an affected child will be produced.

When studying matings among relatives, the inbreeding coefficient is used. The inbreeding coefficient (F) is the probability that a child will be homozygous for a gene derived from a common ancestor of his parents. It is determined by

$$F = (1/2)^n$$

where n is the number of individuals counting from the child to the ancestor and back (but excluding the child). n must be calculated for each common ancestor, and all values of n added together. The proportion of homozygous recessives in the general population can be calculated from

$$p^2 (1 - F) + pF$$

where p is the frequency of the gene in the population.

Problem Solving Examples:

Hardy-Weinberg Principle and Gene Frequency

 What are the implications of the Hardy-Weinberg Law?

The Hardy-Weinberg Law states that in a population at equilibrium, both gene and genotype frequencies remain constant from generation to generation. An equilibrium population refers to a large interbreeding population in which mating is random and no selection or other factor which tends to change gene frequencies occurs.

Mating Male	Female	Frequency	Offspring		
AA	$\times$ AA	$1/4 \times 1/4$	$1/16\,AA$		
AA	$\times$ Aa	$1/4 \times 1/2$	$1/16\,AA$ +	$1/16\,Aa$	
AA	$\times$ aa	$1/4 \times 1/4$		$1/16\,Aa$	
Aa	$\times$ AA	$1/2 \times 1/4$	$1/16\,AA$ +	$1/16\,Aa$	
Aa	$\times$ Aa	$1/2 \times 1/2$	$1/16\,AA$ +	$1/8\,Aa$ +	$1/16\,aa$
Aa	$\times$ aa	$1/2 \times 1/4$		$1/16\,Aa$ +	$1/16\,aa$
aa	$\times$ AA	$1/4 \times 1/4$		$1/16\,Aa$	
aa	$\times$ Aa	$1/4 \times 1/2$		$1/16\,Aa$ +	$1/16\,aa$
aa	$\times$ aa	$1/4 \times 1/4$			$1/16\,aa$
		Sum:	$4/16\,AA$ +	$8/16\,Aa$ +	$4/16\,aa$

Table 8.1 — The offspring of the random mating of a population composed of 1/4 *AA*, 1/2 *Aa*, and 1/4 *aa* individuals

The Hardy-Weinberg Law is a mathematical formulation which resolves the puzzle of why recessive genes do not disappear in a population over time. To illustrate the principle let us look at the distribution in a population of a single gene pair, *A* and *a*. Any member of the population will have the genotype *AA*, *Aa*, or *aa*. If these genotypes are present in the population in the ratio of 1/4 *AA* : 1/2 *Aa* : 1/4 *aa*, we can show that given random mating and comparable viability of progeny in each cross, the genotypes and gene frequencies should remain the same in the next generation. Table 1 shows how the genotypic frequencies of *AA*, *Aa*, and *aa* compare in the population and among the offspring.

Since the genotype frequencies are identical, it follows that the gene frequencies are also the same.

It is very important to realize that the Hardy-Weinberg Law is theoretical in nature and holds true only when factors which tend to change gene frequencies are absent. Examples of such factors are natural selection, mutation, migration, and genetic drift.

Q In a group of students, about 36 percent could roll their tongues, a trait determined by a dominant gene. The other 64 percent of the students were nonrollers. Calculate the frequencies of the gene *R* for tongue rolling and its recessive allele *r* for nonrolling.

 A This problem can be solved by using the Hardy-Weinberg formula.

$$p^2 + 2pq + q^2 = 1$$

Let p = frequency of *R*

q = frequency of *r*

p^2 = frequency of homozygous tongue rollers *RR*

$2pq$ = frequency of heterozygous tongue rollers *Rr*

q^2 = frequency of non-tongue rollers *rr*

The percent of nonrollers was given as 64 percent. Change this to a frequency by moving the decimal two places to the left (0.64).

$q^2 = 0.64$

$q = \sqrt{0.64} = 0.8$ the frequency of r

$p + q = 1$ so $p = 1 - q = 1 - 0.8 = 0.2$ the frequency of R

Q If the frequency of the gene for widow's peak, a dominant trait, is 0.07, what will be the frequency of

(a) persons homozygous for widow's peak,

(b) persons heterozygous for widow's peak, and

(c) persons lacking widow's peak?

A Solve the problem using the Hardy-Weinberg formula.

$p^2 + 2pq + q^2 = 1$

Let p = the frequency of W, $p = 0.07$

q = the frequency of w, $q = 0.93$

$p + q = 1$

so if the frequency for p is known, then q can be readily determined.

$q = 1 - p, q = 1 - .07 = .93$

(a) p^2 = frequency of homozygous widow's peak (WW)

$p^2 = (0.07)^2 = 0.0049$

(b) $2pq$ = frequency of heterozygous widow's peak (Ww)

$2pq = 2(0.07)\,(0.93) = 0.1302$

(c) q^2 = frequency of homozygotes for the recessive gene for no widow's peak

$q^2 = (0.93)^2 = 0.8649$

Q From 146 students tested for PTC tasting ability, 105 were tasters and 41 were non-tasters. Calculate the frequencies of tasters and non-tasters.

A The ability to taste depends upon a dominant gene T. In the Hardy-Weinberg theorem, $p^2 + 2pq + q^2 = 1$, the percentage of non-tasters (tt) may be represented as q^2. Therefore,

$$q^2 = \frac{41}{146} = 0.28$$

$q = \sqrt{.28} = 0.53$ = frequency of t

We can find the frequency of T by substituting it for p in the equation

$p + q = 1$

$p = 1 - q$

$p = 1 - 0.53 = 0.47$ = frequency of T

With the expression $p^2 + 2pq + q^2$, we can calculate the frequencies of TT and Tt tasters.

$TT = p^2 = (0.47)^2 = 0.2209$

$Tt = 2pq = 2(0.47)\,(0.53) = 0.4982$

$tt = q^2 = (0.53)^2 = 0.2809$

We add these up to check our calculations. They should add up to equal 1.

0.2209

0.4982

0.2809
  ___

1.0000

Q In humans, the *M, MN*, and *N* blood groups are determined by two codominant alleles: L^m and L^n. In a population of 800 college students the following phenotypes were identified:

Blood Group	Number
M	392
MN	336
N	72
	___
	800

Determine the frequency of the L^m and L^n alleles.

A Since both alleles can be identified in each individual in which they occur, the frequency of each can be calculated directly.

Let p = frequency of L^m and q = frequency of L^n.

Then

$$p = \frac{\text{total number of } L^m \text{alleles in population}}{\text{total number of genes in population}}$$

and we have,

$$p = \frac{(392 \times 2) + 336}{800 \times 2} = \frac{1,120}{1,600} = 0.7$$

Similarly,

$$q = \frac{\text{total number of } L^n \text{alleles in population}}{\text{total number of genes in population}}$$

and we have

$$q = \frac{(72 \times 2) + 336}{800 \times 2} = \frac{480}{1,600} = 0.3$$

Q Given a population in genetic equilibrium in which the initial gene frequency of d is 0.2; assume the rate of mutation (u) of $D \to d$ to be 4.1×10^{-5}, and the rate of back mutation (v) of $d \to D$ to be 2.5×10^{-7}.

(a) If the above rates of mutation are introduced into the population, what will be the change in q (frequency of d) in the first generation?

(b) Assuming that the above rates continue over time, what will be the value of q at mutational equilibrium?

A (a) If u is the rate of mutation from D to d, and p is the frequency of D, then there will be (u) (p) new d genes after mutation. Similarly, if v is the rate of mutation from d to D, then there will be (v) (q) d genes removed by back mutation. Thus, the new gene frequency, $q_1 = q_0 + up_0 - vq_0$, and the change of gene frequency Δq will be

$$\Delta q = q_1 - q_0 = up_0 - vq_0$$

Therefore,

$$\Delta q = (0.000041)\,(0.8) - (0.00000025)\,(0.2)$$
$$= 0.00003275.$$

(b) At equilibrium, $up = vq$ because $\Delta q = 0$.

Then, the gene frequency,

$$q_e = \frac{u}{u + v}.$$

By substituting in the values for u and v, we get:

$$q_e = \frac{0.000041}{0.00004125} = 0.9939.$$

 Assume a population of garden peas in genetic equilibrium in which the frequencies of the genes for full pods (F) and constricted pods (f) are 0.6 and 0.4, respectively. If this population is allowed only to reproduce by self-fertilization for three generations, what will be the distribution of the three genotypes by the third generation of self-fertilization?

If the population is in a state of genetic equilibrium initially, then the distribution of genotypes before self-fertilization is imposed will be

$$(0.6\,F + 0.4\,f\,)^2 = 0.36\,FF + 0.48\,Ff + 0.16\,ff$$

Self-fertilization, which is the most severe form of inbreeding, will reduce the frequency of heterozygotes by one-half each generation, with the reduction being equally distributed between the two homozygotes.

Thus, the frequencies of these three genotypes will be

generation 1 — 0.48 *FF* + 0.24 *Ff* + 0.28 *ff*

generation 2 — 0.54 *FF* + 0.12 *Ff* + 0.34 *ff*

generation 3 — 0.57 *FF* + 0.06 *Ff* + 0.37 *ff*

Q Consider a population of garden peas in which the genes *F* for full pods and *f* for constricted pods are segregating. Assuming that gene frequencies for this population are found to be: *p* (frequency of *F*) = 0.7 and *q* (frequency of *f*) = 0.3, and that the population is in genetic equilibrium, what proportion of the progeny produced from matings of full-podded × full-podded will be constricted-podded?

A Since the population is in genetic equilibrium, and therefore is undergoing random mating, there are three types of full × full matings:

(a)   *FF* × *FF* which occurs at a frequency of p^4

(b)   *FF* × *Ff* which occurs at a frequency of $4p^3q$ and

(c)   *Ff* × *Ff* which occurs at a frequency of $4p^2q^2$.

Of these, only the *Ff* × *Ff* matings will produce constricted-podded progeny at a frequency of p^2q^2. Thus, the proportion of constricted-podded progeny from full × full matings will be

$$\frac{p^2q^2}{p^4 + 4p^3q + 4p^2q^2}.$$

This can be simplified to

$$\text{proportion } ff \text{ progeny} = \left(\frac{q}{1+q}\right)^2.$$

Now by substituting in the value of q, we get the proportion of

$$ff \text{ progeny} = \left(\frac{0.3}{1.3}\right)^2 = 0.0532.$$

Q Eighty-three monozygotic twin pairs are examined for the presence of club feet. Fifty pairs do not show the trait at all; twenty pairs have one member with club feet; and thirteen pairs have both members affected. What is the frequency of concordance?

A Concordant twins are alike with respect to a particular trait and discordant twins are different. Here, the concordant twins both have club feet. In the discordant pairs, one twin has club feet while the other does not. In identical twins — monozygotes — concordance varies with different traits. A high degree of concordance is due to the twins' genetic identity, to the similarity of their environments or to a combination of both of these factors.

In this problem we are asked to find the concordance frequency for the club foot trait. The frequency of concordance

$$= \frac{\text{number of pairs where both show trait}}{\text{number of pairs where at least one shows trait}}$$

$$= \frac{13}{20+13} = 0.39$$

So these twins are 39 percent concordant for the trait for club feet.

Q Concordance for Down's syndrome in monozygotic twins is not 100 percent. Explain.

 A In about 11 percent of the cases where monozygotic twins have Down's syndrome, one of the twins is normal. This may be due to the loss of one of the three chromosome 21's by one of the two cells formed at the first cleavage. One of the cells would develop into a normal embryo with the proper two copies of each chromosome, and the other would develop into an embryo with three chromosome 21's. Another possibility is shown in the diagram. If somatic nondisjunction occurred at an early cell division of one of the twins, then that twin would develop Down's syndrome.

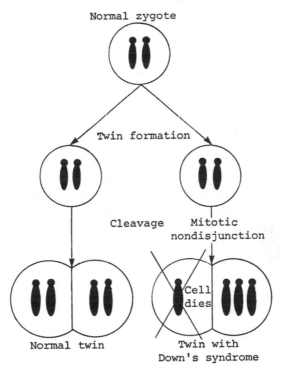

Figure 8.1

In a plant breeding experiment, cross-fertilization can cause a marked increase in the yield and height of the plants. Explain.

In cross-breeding experiments the progeny are very often more vigorous than the parents. This is called heterosis. Heterosis has been explained by two theories. The first is called the dominance hypothesis. This assumes that in the course of selecting for certain desirable traits the breeder has created strains with somewhat deleterious recessive genes in other places along the genome. The hybrid formed between two inbred strains would be heterozygous at these loci and hence would show vigor that the parents did not show.

The second hypothesis regarding heterosis is called the overdominance hypothesis. This theory says that the hybrid is more vigorous because it is more heterozygous. Heterozygotes may be more flexible than homozygotes since they have two different alleles for their heterozygous genes. The heterozygote may be better able to survive fluctuations in its environment since it has two versions of its heterozygous genes and, hence, two versions of the gene products.

Heterosis has been used to increase crop yields and disease resistance in some plants such as corn and sorghum wheat.

CHAPTER 9

Genetic Material

The structure of DNA is best appreciated by looking at the functions that it performs.

1. It must be able to replicate itself.

2. It must contain the information to direct growth and development.

The structural simplicity of DNA seems to make it an unlikely candidate for such important jobs. However, the process of **transformation**—the conversion of an organism's phenotype to another form—provides evidence for the chemical basis of inheritance. By way of review, DNA contains two deoxyribose-phosphate sidechains and four nitrogenous bases arranged in hydrogen-bonded pairs.

The basis for understanding DNA replication and protein synthesis is the complementarity of these bases. Adenine always pairs with thymine, and guanine always pairs with cytosine, because of their physical and chemical fit. The double-ringed purines, adenine and guanine, fit between the sugar-phosphate backbones when bonded to the single-ringed pyrimidines, thymine and cytosine. Chemically, adenine and thymine form two hydrogen bonds, while guanine and cytosine form three.

The number of bases is characteristic for a particular species. Because of the complementarity of bases, we can use the percentage of one base to determine the percentage of all bases. The percentage of one base equals the percentage of its complement. Subtract these percentages from 100 percent to get the total of the other two bases. Divide this total by two to find the percentage of each of the last two bases.

Alternatively, the base content of one strand can be used to calculate the base content of the other. Using the fact that adenine (a) = thymine (t) and guanine (g) = cytosine (c), the $a + g$ / $t + c$ content for one strand is the same for the other. Also, the $a + t$ / $g + c$ content for one strand equals the $g + c$ / $a + t$ for the complementary strand.

The process of replication is also based upon complementarity. When the two DNA strands uncoil, each base can only hydrogen bond with its complement. Therefore, in determining the base sequence for the new strand, a pairs with t, t with a, g with c, and c with g.

Replication, as with other chemical reactions, is under enzymatic control. It may be easier to follow the events in replication by listing the enzymes and other proteins needed and defining the role of each. The list should include: DNA B protein, primase, rep protein, SSB protein, gyrase, DNA polymerase III holoenzyme, DNA polymerase I, and ligase.

Various genetic units have been defined in the past. It is helpful to get a sense of their sizes to understand what portion of the genome they represent. The terms cistron, muton, and recon should be defined first; then the number of nucleotides they contain can be determined.

When looking for experimental evidence that indicates that genes control amino acid sequences in proteins, it is important to look at proteins that have been sequenced, such as insulin and hemoglobin. Other valuable information comes from mutations in the genes that alter specific amino acids.

Protein synthesis requires RNA as well as DNA. Understanding their roles begins with a familiarity with their structures. RNA is different from DNA in that it is single-stranded and contains ribose instead of deoxyribose, and uracil instead of thymine.

Knowing the functions of each RNA (m-RNA, r-RNA, t-RNA) helps in understanding the range of variability for each. Messenger RNA is the RNA template for the protein coding genes. The number of mRNAs reflects the number of proteins a cell makes. The cloverleaf structure of transfer RNA allows for amino acid attachment and anticodons (that recognize the mRNA codon). Each amino acid must have its own transfer RNA in order for it to translate the mRNA message. Ribosomal RNA is the factory for many syntheses, and, therefore, does not have to be uniquely structured.

In determining the time of DNA and RNA production, radioactive precursors are used. If you were to predict the time for these events, you would think about the fact that the chromosomes must be uncoiled, as in interphase. Also, realize that the same template is needed for both events; therefore, they should occur at different times.

While both DNA strands are necessary for replication, only one strand is needed for protein synthesis. The latter is called the **sense strand**, and its complement is called the **nonsense strand**. The sense strand acts as a template to make its complement, mRNA. Therefore, the base sequence of the sense strand can be used to determine the mRNA base sequence. Care should be taken to pair DNA's adenine with RNA's uracil.

Protein synthesis is a multistep process. It may be easier to follow by looking at transcription and translation separately. Transcription is mRNA production and is mediated by RNA polymerase. When thinking about the role of RNA polymerase, remember that the DNA strands must be uncoiled to expose the sense strand and the RNA nucleotides must be aligned for base pairing and bonding between sugars and phosphates.

For translation, be careful to distinguish between initiation, elongation, and termination. For initiation you should remember the initiation factors, the source of energy needed for attachment of the first mRNA codon, the attachment site on the ribosome, and the initiator codon. When thinking about elongation, review the role of the *P* and *A* sites on the ribosome as well as the function of peptidyl transferase. For more detail, the roles of GTP and elongation factors should be included. When reviewing termination, the role of releasing factors as well as terminator codons should be examined.

When reviewing the breaking of the genetic code it is important to remember that test tube systems can be set up. Ribosomes can be extracted from cells. Also, different kinds of mRNA can be synthesized. And, finally, amino acids can be added post-translationally. The proteins that are formed can be extracted and analyzed for their amino acid sequence.

One should also realize that at least one codon must exist for each amino acid. Since there are 20 amino acids, there must be at least 20 codons. You can predict the number of combinations of four bases possible by taking two at a time vs. three at a time, by multiplying 4×4 vs. $4 \times 4 \times 4$.

If the DNA sense strand is known, we can predict its mRNA code and polypeptide sequence, and also predict the effects of a mutation. Rewrite the DNA sense strand in mutant form. Make new mRNA from it, and translate the new strand into its amino acid sequence by looking up the codons on a genetic code chart.

We can also determine how mutations might have occurred when one amino acid is replaced by another. Look up all possible codons for each amino acid, and look for what changes in the original codon would result in a codon for the observed new amino acid.

When judging the effects of a base substitution on protein structure and function, remember that it can cause a change in a codon. This results in a single amino acid change. To judge the kinds of changes in function possible, remember that the chemistry of amino acids depends upon the nature of their ions—the presence of and kind of charge, and whether they are hydrophilic or hydrophobic. A change in the chemistry at one amino acid site could alter the shape of the protein or affect the ability of an active site to function.

Problem Solving Examples:

DNA and RNA

 What are the nitrogen-containing bases that are part of DNA and RNA? Draw the structures indicating which are purines and which are pyrimidines.

Purines

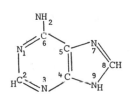

Adenine

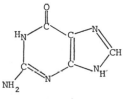

Guanine

Pyrimidines

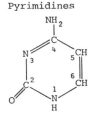

Cytosine

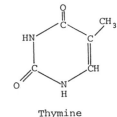

Thymine

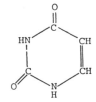

Uracil

Figure 9.1

DNA and RNA are made up of sugar moieties, phosphate groups, and nitrogenous bases. It is the bases which encode the genetic information. DNA can contain the purines, adenine and guanine, and the pyrimidines, cytosine and thymine. RNA contains uracil instead of thymine. Uracil is also a pyrimidine. Notice that purines contain two rings and pyrimidines have one ring.

 Draw a molecular diagram of the mRNA that would be transcribed by the sequence ATA in the sense strand of a molecule of DNA.

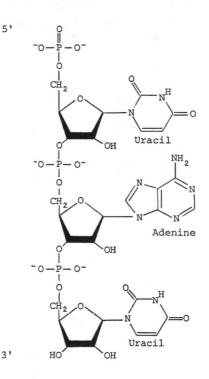

Figure 9.2

Ribonucleic acid (RNA) differs from DNA in three important ways: RNA contains the sugar ribose instead of deoxyribose; RNA has uracil instead of thymine; and RNA is single-stranded. RNA's backbone, like that of DNA, is held together by phosphodiester bonds. The mRNA molecule has the complementary sequence UAU as shown in the diagram.

 RNA is readily hydrolized by alkali, but DNA is not. Why?

A RNA and DNA have different chemical structures. RNA has uracil instead of thymine and it is single, rather than double-stranded. But most importantly for this problem, it has ribose as its sugar moiety. Ribose has two hydroxyl (-OH) groups while DNA's sugar, deoxyribose, has only one. This extra hydroxyl group is not bound up in the phosphodiester bond and is free to react (see Figure 9.3).

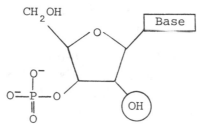

Figure 9.3

When alkali is added to a solution containing RNA, this hydroxyl group is ionized. It can then act as an intramolecular catalyst to cause the formation of a 2′–3′ cyclic intermediate with the adjacent phosphate group. This reaction disrupts the phosphodiester bond, thus breaking the backbone of the molecule. Since DNA does not have this free hydroxyl group, it is not as readily disrupted by alkaline treatment.

 A DNA molecule has 180 base pairs and is 20 percent adenine. How many cytosine nucleotides are present in this molecule of DNA?

 In DNA, the complementary pairing between bases is always $A - T (T - A)$ and $G - C (C - G)$. Thus, if 20 percent of the nucleotides are adenine, then the total composition of $A - T$ will be 40 percent, and the total composition of $G - C$ will be 60 percent. The amount of cytosine will be 30 percent, or 108 nucleotides ($360 \times 0.30 = 108$).

 Given the following molecule of DNA:

strand 1 —— 5′ *A A A T C G A T T G G C A C A* —— 3′
strand 2 —— 3′ *T T T A G C T A A C C G T G T* —— 5′

Assuming that strand 1 will serve as the transcription template, construct the molecule of mRNA that will be transcribed.

 Since RNA has U instead of T, the complementary pairing that will occur in transcription is A of DNA with U of RNA and T of DNA with A of RNA. Thus, the mRNA molecule that will be transcribed from the above DNA strand 1 will be

—— 3′ *U U U A G C U A A C C G U G U* 5′ ——

 Given the following DNA transcription template for an mRNA molecule:

—— *A A C G T A T T C A A C T C A* ——

What will be the polypeptide sequence if a transition mutation occurs to the G nucleotide? How will it differ from the normal polypeptide sequence?

First, we must determine what the normal polypeptide sequence will be. This we can do by constructing the mRNA molecule, which will be

— *U U G C A U A A G U U G A G U* —

The normal polypeptide sequence will include the following amino acids:

— *leu – his – lys – leu – ser* —

Now a transition mutation for *G* would result in the substitution of an *A* for the *G*, which would change the second codon for the mutant mRNA from *CAU* to *UAU*. This change would result in the substitution of the amino acid tyrosine (tyr) for histidine (his) in the polypeptide sequence.

Q Why and how do circular molecules of DNA become supercoiled?

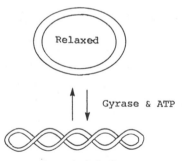

Figure 9.4

A Circular molecules can become supercoiled by the action of gyrase in the presence of ATP. Supercoiled DNA has a more compact shape than the uncoiled (relaxed) DNA molecule so more DNA molecules can be packed into a small space. Supercoiling can also influence the degree of unwinding of the double helix; negative supercoiling can result in an uncoiling of the double helix. This may aid in exposing the strands to replication and transcription enzymes, thus allowing those processes to occur.

Genes

 What experimental evidence indicates that genes control the amino acid sequences in proteins?

In 1953, the first amino acid sequence of a protein was completed. After six years, Frederick Sanger had succeeded in sequencing the amino acid sequence of a relatively small protein, insulin. He used different proteolytic enzymes to cleave the protein molecule into fragments that could be sequenced more easily than the large molecule. Many of the fragments had overlapping sequences, so the linear order of the whole insulin molecule could be pieced together. This showed that the amino acid sequence is what individualizes proteins. Insulin is insulin because of its specific amino acid sequence.

Vernon Ingram chose a well-studied inherited disorder, sickle-cell anemia. In 1957, he sequenced normal hemoglobin (HbA) and sickled hemoglobin (HbS). He compared the amino acid sequences and found a difference of one amino acid. This connected the abnormal amino acid sequence of a protein to an inherited, and hence, genetic disorder.

Ingram's discovery was proof that a mutation in a gene resulted in an abnormal amino acid sequence in a protein. But, as in almost all experimentation, he had to use techniques pioneered by others. The sequencing technique developed by Sanger was very important in the determination of a link between genes and amino acid sequences in proteins.

Transcription and Translation

What are enhancer sequences?

Enhancers are DNA sequences that bind transcription factors, also called enhancer binding proteins. Enhancers can be located near the gene, within it or as far as several kilobases away. They are orientation independent as well as position independent. The enhancer complement of a gene determines both its level of expression and its tissue specificity. Many enhancer binding proteins are activated or inactivated during cell signalling, making the gene hormone-responsive. Different genes in a cell can be turned on by different hormonal stimulation by virtue of different enhancers for different genes. The same hormone can induce the expression of different genes in different target cells as a result of differences in the enhancer-binding-protein population within the various cell types.

How is protein synthesis initiated?

Messenger RNA molecules are translated to proteins at the ribosomes. At their 5′ ends, the mRNAs have a leader sequence. This "cap" contains a methyl-guanosyl triphosphate group which binds to the small ribosomal subunit. In eukaryotes, the association of ribosome, mRNA and tRNA requires three protein factors called initiation factors — IF–1, IF–2, and IF–3. IF–3 is necessary for the binding of the ribosome to mRNA. Once bound, the other two initiation factors and the hydrolysis of GTP is required for the binding of the first codon of the mRNA to the small ribosome. When the initiation factors are released, the large ribosomal subunit attaches. The complete ribosome has two sites for tRNA molecules, the peptidyl (*P*) site and the aminoacyl (*A*) site. The mRNA codons are held near these spots so the tRNAs can bind.

The initiation is complete and the machinery is poised for elongation of the polypeptide chain.

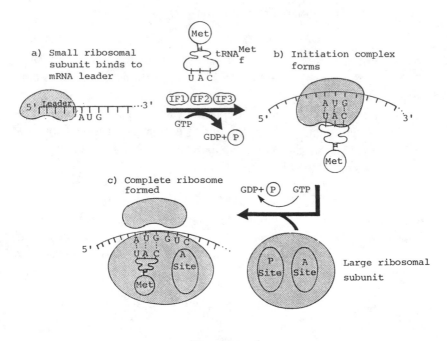

Figure 9.5

Genetic Code

Q If an mRNA molecule synthesized in the laboratory consists only of adenine and guanine in an approximate 2:1 ratio, what possible amino acids could be included in the polypeptide to be produced?

A Since the only nucleotides present are adenine (*A*) and guanine (*G*), then only those amino acids coded for by codons possessing any combination of *A* and/or *G* will be present. There are four amino acids that fit such a requirement: lysine (*lys*), arginine (*arg*), glutamic acid (*glu*), and glycine (*gly*). Further, since the ratio of *A:G* is 2:1 in this molecule, it is likely that any numerical repetition of the combination of the following five codons will suffice:

AAA (*lys*), *AAG* (*lys*), *AGA* (*arg*), *GAA* (*glu*), and *GGA* (*gly*).

CHAPTER 10

Bacterial and Viral Genetics

When studying the genetics of bacteria, you must distinguish between three mechanisms of transfer: conjugation, transformation, and transduction. **Conjugation** is the transfer of genetic material from donor to recipient bacteria through a sex pilus. During **transformation**, bacteria pick up DNA fragments from the environment. For **transduction**, bacteriophage carry genetic material from donor bacteria to recipient bacteria. For viruses, exchanges of genetic material occur when two strains infect the same cell.

To better understand conjugation in bacteria, you should know that they contain a single circular chromosome as well as smaller autonomous genetic elements called **plasmids**. The F^+ factor codes for the formation of the sex pilus, and is easily transferred to recipient cells in its plasmid form. This transfer to F^- cells occurs with little recombination. When the F^+ is inserted in the main chromosome, many recombinants appear among the F^- recipients. These Hfrs (high frequency recombinants) can be used to map genes on the main chromosome.

During a cross, the main chromosome of the Hfr cell breaks and threads through the pilus into the F^- recipient. Interrupting conjugation by shaking the cells at different times allows varying amounts of the chromosome to pass to the recipient. The transferred chromosomal fragment plus its recipient creates a partial diploid (merozygote) and provides the opportunity for recombination. Genes can be mapped by the amount of time it takes for genes to transfer.

In addition to the F^+ factor, other plasmids also exist. Those carrying genes for drug resistance can easily transfer to F^- recipients during conjugation. When new drug-resistant phenotypes appear in a population, plasmid transfer by conjugation or transformation might be the cause. Remember that mutation is a relatively infrequent event.

Transformation is also an effective mapping tool for bacteria, since the merozygotes that form can undergo recombination. In determining whether two genes are linked we can use double mutants as recipients. Let's use two different donors, each containing a single mutant at the same time, and let's assume that the genes in question are linked. Double transformants (two wild-type genes) would occur less frequently than single transformants (one wild-type gene), since the former would be due to the transfer of two pieces of DNA rather than one. If we use a donor containing two wild-type genes, double transformants would occur more frequently than single transformants, since single transformants would be due to recombination. If the genes are not linked the results of both crosses would be about the same.

To determine map distances between two genes, you might transform double mutant recipients with a donor containing only wild-type genes. Recombination between the genes results in two different single transformants (one wild phenotype). Divide the sum of single transformants by the total number of transformations (both single and double) for the recombination frequency.

When using transduction for mapping bacterial genomes, we must be familiar with bacteriophage, viruses that act as vectors in such transfers. The viral infection may initiate two events.

1. Viral genetic material enters the cell and replicates. The host cell lysis releasing new viral particles.

2. Viral genetic material (DNA or a DNA copy of viral RNA) is incorporated into the host genome, in many cases at a specific site. This phenomenon is called **lysogeny**. The viral material (called the **prophage**) may be carried through many host cell divisions before separating from the genome and lysing the host to release new viral particles.

Each process of lysis has the potential to incorporate and transfer host DNA. In the first case, the host DNA may become fragmented as part of lysis and some of the fragments may become incorporated into viral protein coats. Any piece of DNA may be transferred in this way, and the process is, therefore, called generalized transduction.

In the second case, specialized transduction, the prophage separates from its host and may carry a neighboring portion of the host genome with it. Where incorporation of the virus is at a specific site, only certain host genes may be transferred by the virus.

The transduced DNA may be incorporated into the recipient genome by recombination. If not incorporated (abortive transduction), it does not replicate with the rest of the genome, but passes to only one cell at each division. In determining whether growth of this cell line will occur, look at the genotype of this merozygote and see if the medium provides the nutrients that are required. When predicting the amount of growth possible, realize that only one cell in each generation will get the fragment.

Transduction can be used to map the distance between two bacterial genes by using the formula

$$\frac{\text{\# single recombinants}}{\text{total recombinants}}$$

where the total recombinants equals the sum of the double recombinants plus the single recombinants.

You can also use transduction data to determine the sequence of genes transduced. Let's assume a phage transduces three genes to a recipient containing alleles of those genes. If we select for one or two of the transduced alleles on the appropriate medium, the frequency with which the other (unselected) alleles are also found increases as their genes get closer.

If we have two strains of a particular organism that carry phenotypically similar mutants, we might want to know if the mutants are alleles of the same gene or are due to two different genes. Remember that two different genes would complement each other when both are present. For bacteria, this would occur in merozygotes. To form merozygotes, choose the appropriate form of gene transfer based upon the strains available. For example, in order to use conjugation you must have an F^+ strain carrying one mutant and an F^- strain carrying the other mutant.

The same test for complementation can be done with two mutant strains of virus. When both infect the same cell, a wild phenotype would occur if each mutant is the result of a separate gene. If the two mutants are alleles of the same gene, then neither strain would have that functioning gene.

Mutations in the rII region of T4 phage have been studied extensively. Wild-type phage can lyse strains B and K of *E. coli*, while mutations in the rII region result in inability to lyse strain K. When two mutants infect the same strain B cell, recombination can occur. Recombinants can be detected by plating on a lawn of strain K cells; the wild-type recombinants would cause lysis. The distance between two mutants is expressed as the recombination frequency using the following:

$$\% \text{ recombination} = \frac{\# \text{ plaques that form on } K}{\# \text{ plaques that form on } B} \times 100\%$$

Before plating viruses, the viral suspension is diluted by varying amounts. Be sure to adjust the plaque number on the lawn of strain *K* so that it reflects the same dilution as that used on the lawn of strain *B*.

To narrow down the location of a point mutation more easily, it can be crossed with strains of T4 phage containing deletions. If the point mutation occurs in the same region as the deletion, recombination will not produce a wild-type phenotype.

When several point mutations are crossed with different deletion mutants, we can map the point mutations in relationship to each other. Start with a deletion that covers all but one point mutation. That mutation would be outside the deletion region and at one end of our map. Look for another deletion that either includes our first point mutation plus one other, or excludes the first plus one other. Thus, the second point mutation can be mapped next to the first. Continue examining all deletions.

It is worth noting here that viruses infect not only prokaryotic cells but also eukaryotic cells. They use the host's protein-making machinery for production of new viral particles. For RNA viruses, reverse transcriptase must first produce a DNA copy, which is used to make new RNA viral genomes and viral proteins. Interferon, a product of the immune system, may interfere with the ability of viral mRNA to bind to ribosomes, and, thus, interfere with viral protein synthesis.

Problem Solving Examples:

Bacterial Genetics

 What are some advantages of doing genetics in bacteria and yeast instead of in larger organisms (i.e., multicellular eukaryotes)?

 Most of the biochemical pathway archetypes have been worked out in bacteria, mainly through mutant analysis. A typical approach for a researcher to take to study a particular pathway is to study mutants defective in that process. Such defects usually involve one of the genes encoding a protein that participates in the pathway or regulates it. The probability that any given individual organism has such a mutation is very low, meaning that several organisms must be screened to find mutants of interest. Knockout mutations of any given single gene occur at frequencies of about 10^{-5} to 10^{-6} (in bacteria), while change-of-function mutations occur at frequencies 10 to 100 times lower. Bacteria can be grown to large numbers quickly (overnight), inexpensively, and in a small space. Because cultures of 10^8 organisms are required to get a usable number of mutants, it is easy to see why many geneticists work with bacteria instead of larger forms of life.

Ploidy is another reason for using a prokaryotic organism. Prokaryotes are haploid, having only one copy of each locus. Eukaryotes on the other hand are diploid; each chromosome, and hence each locus, has a homolog. Therefore, most mutant phenotypes require inactivation of both loci. The frequency of double inactivation is the square of the frequency of a single inactivation, making such events prohibitively rare. It is, however, more difficult to determine the nature of the mutant (dominant vs. recessive) in a haploid system.

The yeasts are also very useful experimental organisms. They retain many of the benefits of prokaryotes, yet are eukaryotic and thus more closely related to larger, multicellular animals and plants. They are also useful for studying penetrance and dominance/recessivity questions. Yeast can be grown in either the haploid or diploid state and can be readily interconverted. Many core eukaryotic pathways have been worked out in yeast. The cell division cycle, recombination, and models of gene expression are all examples of eukaryotic paradigms worked out in yeast.

How do bacteria develop drug resistance?

Most antibiotic resistant bacteria result from genetic changes and subsequent selection. The genetic changes may be due to chromosomal mutations or to the introduction of extra chromosomal elements.

Spontaneous mutations in a bacterial chromosome can cause antibiotic resistance in several forms. The mutation may make the cell impermeable to the drug by changing the shape of the receptor molecule. The mutation may create an enzyme that inactivates the drug once it enters the cell. The mutation may make the drug's intercellular targets resistant to the drug. Streptomycin, which inhibits the binding of formyl-methionyl tRNA to the ribosomes, may be blocked if the ribosome was changed so that the interaction was prevented.

Antibiotic resistance may also arise extrachromosomally. Conjugal plasmids, such as R plasmids, contain genes which mediate their genetic transmission. R plasmids carry genes conferring antibiotic resistance. Thus, R^+ cells can pass the genes for resistance to R^- cells by conjugation.

Once a bacterial cell strain has become resistant to an antibiotic, the presence of that antibiotic in the environment favors the cells that contain the resistance element. Cells without the resistance will be killed by the antibiotic; those that have the resistance will flourish.

In Japan, the frequency of the R-governed multiple drug-resistant strain of *Shigella*, which causes dysentery, rose from 0.2 percent in 1953 to 58 percent in 1965. Also, 84 percent of the *E. coli* and 90 percent of *Proteus* collected from affected hospital patients showed similar resistance. How could such an increase happen?

All three strains contain an *R* plasmid in this example. *R* plasmids carry genes for conjugal transfer and genes for antibiotic resistance. The antibiotic genes are contained within larger units called transposons. Transposons are short segments of DNA which cannot self-replicate. They persist by inserting into a chromosome or plasmid and being replicated along with the host DNA. They can hop (transpose) from one plasmid to another or from one site on the plasmid to another site on the same plasmid. *R* plasmids can pick up additional transposons, so they can acquire resistance to more antibiotics.

R plasmids can be transmitted from cell to cell and even from cells of one species to those of another. Thus, if nonpathogenic bacterial strains, such as *E. coli* and *Proteus*, obtain an *R* plasmid they can spread it to other bacteria, their own kind as well as infectious pathogenic strains. Normally, the *R* factor is passed at a very low frequency. However, the indiscriminate use of antibiotics in medicine and agriculture has selected for drug-resistant enterobacteria (bacteria which live in the intestinal tract and aid the digestion). These bacteria can then pass their resistance to potentially harmful strains. The use of antibiotics should be moderated to prevent the spread of resistant pathogenic bacteria.

 How is a bacterial zygote different from a eukaryotic zygote?

 A eukaryotic zygote is formed by the fusion of two haploid gametes. True cell fusion does not take place in bacteria and the genetic exchange is not reciprocal as in eukaryotes. Instead, one cell donates some of its genetic information to a recipient cell. The recipient is temporarily diploid for the genes that have been transferred. Such cells are partial zygotes or merozygotes. The genes then incorporate into the cell's chromosome. Any extraneous fragments of DNA are lost from the cell line in subsequent divisions. The clones are once again haploid.

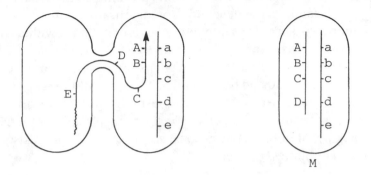

Figure 10.1 — A merozygote (M) formed by the transfer of genes A, B, C, and D from one bacterium to another by conjugation

   The following Hfr strains of *E. coli* donate the markers shown in the order given.

Hfr strain	Marker order
1	*TLPAM*
2	*SGHMA*
3	*RIXSG*
4	*RTLPA*

All of these Hfr strains were obtained from the same *F⁺* strain. What was the order of the markers on the *E. coli F⁺* chromosome?

This problem involves the mapping technique that utilizes bacterial conjugation to find the order of chromosomal markers. The markers occur in different combinations in the donors because the conjugation was disrupted at different times. Since the genetic information is transmitted linearly, the order is not changed. To find the order in the complete circular chromosome, we simply have to fit the fragments together by examining the overlapping areas.

TLPAM

AMHGS

GSXIR

RTLPA

Notice that the first and the last fragments overlap. This is because the chromosome is circular. The complete map of these markers is

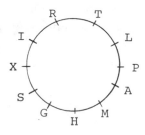

Figure 10.2

Transformation

 What is transformation?

Transformation is a means by which genetic information is passed in bacterial cells. The recipient cell takes up the DNA that has been released by the donor cell. This occurs naturally in some species; however, it is usually performed as part of an experimental procedure. The DNA is extracted from the donor cell and mixed with recipient cells. *Hemophilus influenzae* and *Bacillus*

subtilis are naturally competent; they are capable of taking up high molecular weight DNA from the medium. Competent cells have a surface protein called competence factor, which binds DNA to the cell surface. Other cells, such as *E. coli*, cannot readily undergo transformation. They will only pick up extracellular DNA under special laboratory conditions. The cells must have mutations that stop exonuclease I and V activity. The cells must be treated with high $CaCl_2$ concentrations to make their membranes permeable to the DNA, and the donor DNA must be present in very high concentrations.

The DNA that is picked up by the recipient cell must be double-stranded. As it enters the cell, an intracellular DNAase degrades one of the strands. This hydrolysis provides the energy needed to pull the rest of the DNA into the cell. Once inside the cell, the now single-stranded DNA can insert into homologous regions of the recipient's chromosome. When the donor DNA and recipient DNA have genetic mutations that act as markers, genetic linkage can be established through transformation experiments.

Transduction

Q A *gal⁺/gal⁻* cell is produced by an abortive transduction. Will it grow in a medium in which galactose is the sole carbon source?

A Abortive transductants are cells in which the transduced chromosome fragment does not incorporate into the recipient chromosome through recombination. This may occur when the donor phage comes from a mutant cell which is functionally different than the recipient. Since the fragment contains the genes that are selected for, its presence is essential for a cell's survival. The fragment is not replicated with the rest of the genome because it has not been incorporated. It is passed in unilinear form to one cell at each division. The one cell that has the fragment's genes is prototrophic in the selective media. The cells without it can only undergo a few divisions. A very small colony results from the limited growth of the sibling cells.

Thus, in the *gal⁺/gal⁻* abortive, only the cell with the fragment will produce the galactose-fermenting enzyme. The other cells will be able to use the excess enzyme. Limited growth will continue until the demand for enzyme is greater than the production ability of the one cell. The resulting colony is minute.

CHAPTER 11

Biochemistry and Regulation

To understand biochemical genetics we must be familiar with how chemical reactions occur in the cell. These reactions depend upon the acquisition of nutrient precursors that are converted to various intermediates and, finally, to an end-product. The reactions are mediated by specific enzymes. Any step can be altered if the gene for that enzyme is defective or missing. Modification of any step carries through to all subsequent steps.

We can measure the effects of a particular gene mutant by the amount of precursor, end-product, or enzyme present, or by measuring enzyme activity. Enzyme deficiency diseases are due to recessive genes, since the presence of at least one copy of the normal gene is enough to produce a normal phenotype. When detecting carriers of the recessive gene (heterozygotes), remember that one normal gene will produce a certain amount of normal enzyme, while two normal genes will produce roughly twice as much.

We can determine the sequence of intermediates in a biochemical pathway by using mutant strains of an organism that affect specific steps. Let's assume there are three enzymatic reactions in the pathway. If the mutant strain cannot perform the first reaction, then none of the intermediates or end-product will form. For the mutant strain that cannot perform the second reaction, there will be a buildup of only the first intermediate. For the mutant strain that cannot perform the third reaction, the first two intermediates will accumulate, but no end-product. We can test for the presence of these chemicals in microorganisms by plating them on a minimal medium instead of on a medium that contains nutritional supplements. Then we can determine the step in the pathway that a mutant affects by the supplement(s) required for growth.

In addition to structural genes that code for proteins or transfer and ribosomal RNA, **regulator genes** also exist. These regulator genes either enhance the transcription of structural genes (positive control) or inhibit transcription (negative control).

When looking at regulation in prokaryotes, keep in mind that the structural genes for a particular biochemical pathway are located in sequence next to each other. You should also be familiar with the regulatory genes:

1. The repressor gene produces a repressor protein that binds on the operator to inhibit transcription. When the substrate to be catabolized by the gene product is present, it binds with the repressor protein and prevents repressor inhibition of transcription. For anabolic reactions, the repressor is inactive until it combines with a metabolic end-product; the active repressor, then, binds to the operator preventing further synthesis. Since the repressor protein is a cytoplasmic product, it can act on genes that are on the same chromosome (cis) or on different chromosomes (trans).

2. The operator site is located next to the structural genes. When bound to the repressor protein, RNA polymerase cannot bind. Thus, transcription cannot occur. The operator has its effect on the structural genes distal to it on the same chromosome.

3. The promoter region is located next to the operator site, and is the attachment site for RNA polymerase. Attachment is enhanced in the presence of catabolite activator protein (CAP) and cyclic AMP. The promoter region has its effect on its neighboring operator and structural genes.

When solving problems involving prokaryote regulation, draw a map of the structural and regulatory genes, and list all symbols for mutants with their description. The following symbols are useful to know:

+ = wild type,

− = mutant,

c = constitutive (always functioning).

Remember that the repressor gene can operate in both cis and trans positions, while the promoter and operator regions only operate in cis.

Evidence also exists for regulation in viruses. Regulation in lambda phage determines whether it will undergo lysis or lysogeny. Lysis depends upon the production of new protein coats and replication of the chromosome, while lysogeny involves the incorporation of viral DNA into the host genome. In this viral genome, DNA strands function as sense strands, one reading to the right and the other to the left.

To follow transcription in lambda phage, begin by making a list of its genes, including their functions. Draw two maps of the genome, one to show regulation for lysis and the other for lysogeny. Number the genes in order of transcription for each process. Refer to these maps when asked how the deletion of a gene will affect lysis or lysogeny.

The study of eukaryotic regulation is much more complex, because many eukaryotes are multicellular and have diploid genomes. In addition, eukaryotic genes have introns (intervening sequences) that are excised from the mRNA and never translated.

Experimental evidence exists for hormonal regulation of gene action. Remember the effects of gibberellic acid on seed germination, ecdysone on chromosome puffing patterns in *Drosophila*, and estrogen on transcription. You should also realize that regulation of protein synthesis can occur after transcription.

Problem Solving Examples:

Biochemical Genetics

Q What is the genetic basis of albinism?

A Albinism is characterized by a failure to form the black pigment melanin. Normally, melanin is formed from the product of the hydroxylation of tyrosine. This product, L-dihydroxyphenylalanine, or dopa, is converted to melanin in a series of reactions by the enzyme complex tyrosinase. These reactions occur in melanocytes. Albinos have the normal number of melanocytes in their skin, but tyrosinase activity is not evident.

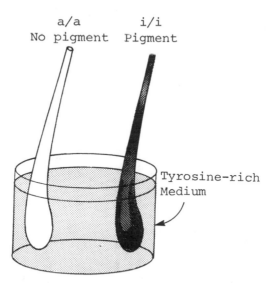

Albinism can result from two different mutant recessive genes. Gene *a* fails to code for the enzyme necessary to convert tyrosine products into melanin; gene *i* prevents normal absorption of tyrosine. When hair, including roots, is cultured in a tyrosine-rich medium, the homozygous *a/a* still fails to produce pigment but homozygous *i/i* does produce pigment.

Figure 11.1

There are a number of genes that are involved in determining the amount of pigment deposited in the skin, hair, and eye cells. This accounts for the great variability in human coloring. However, only one gene locus is involved in the production of melanin. A person who is homozygous for the recessive allele of this gene, which codes for the enzyme that converts tyrosine to dopa, cannot produce melanin.

Albinism can be caused by another genetic factor. Melanin production is dependent on the presence of tyrosine in a cell. A person who is homozygous for an allele at a different locus, will not have membranes permeable to tyrosine. People with this type of albinism have a small amount of melanin due to the creation of phenylalanine from tyrosine that occurs inside the cell. A test for this type of albinism is shown in Figure 11.1.

 How does the measurement of enzymatic activity help to detect galactosemia?

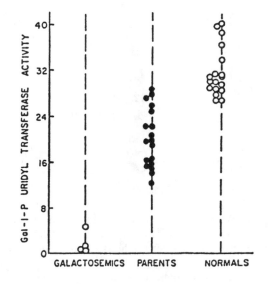

Figure 11.2

Galactosemia is an inherited disorder in which dietary galactose accumulates because its metabolism is blocked. The absence of the enzyme galactose 1-phosphate uridyl transferase blocks the metabolism of galactose. This enzyme is usually present in such large amounts that a 50 percent reduction does not produce clinical symptoms. Heterozygotes have between 60 and 70 percent of the enzymatic activity and thus show no symptoms (see Figure 11. 2). Homozygotes, however, produce no enzyme and usually fail to thrive. When milk is consumed, the affected infants vomit or have diarrhea. Many are mentally retarded. The absence of galactose 1-phosphate uridyl transferase in the red blood cells is a definitive test for the disease.

This disease can be treated with a diet that excludes galactose. Almost all of the clinical symptoms, except for the mental retardation, regress with a galactose-free diet.

Tay-Sachs disease is an inborn error of metabolism. How can heterozygotes be detected?

Tay-Sachs disease is a recessive disease in which the nervous system degenerates. Most affected individuals do not live past age three. Homozygous recessives do not produce the enzyme b-N-acetylhexosaminidase. This enzyme is responsible for the removal of the terminal sugar of one type of lipid. This ganglioside, as it is called, accumulates in the cerebral cortex causing striking pathological changes.

The absence of the enzyme can be detected prenatally by amniocentesis. Heterozygous parents can be detected since the enzyme is only present in 50 percent of the normal amount.

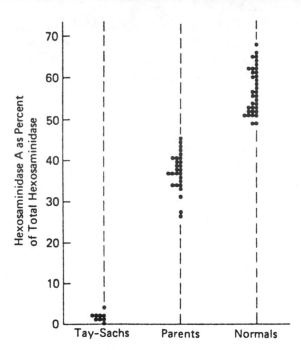

The detection of heterozygotes for the recessive allele causing Tay-Sachs disease. The percentage of hexosaminidase A is very low in affected children, and lower in their parents (who must be heterozygotes) than in normal individuals.

Figure 11.3

 When a person eats food containing phenylalanine or tyrosine, his urine turns black when exposed to air. Explain.

 This condition is due to an inherited metabolic disorder called alcaptonuria. This disorder is another inborn error of metabolism; it is caused by an inherited defect in a single enzyme. The enzyme that is defective in alcaptonuria is homogentisate oxidase.

A person who is homozygous for the recessive allele at the alcaptonuria gene produces urine that turns black because he lacks the enzyme that converts homogentisate to acetoacetate in the phenylalanine and tyrosine catabolic pathway (see Figure 11.4). An fected individual excretes homogentisate into his urine. Homogentisate is oxidized and polymerized to a melanin-like compound when it remains exposed to air. This gives the urine its black color.

Alcaptonuria is relatively benign. It has no very harmful effects in young people. However, later in life it usually results in degenerative arthritis. This may be caused by the crystallization of homogentisate in the cartilages of the body.

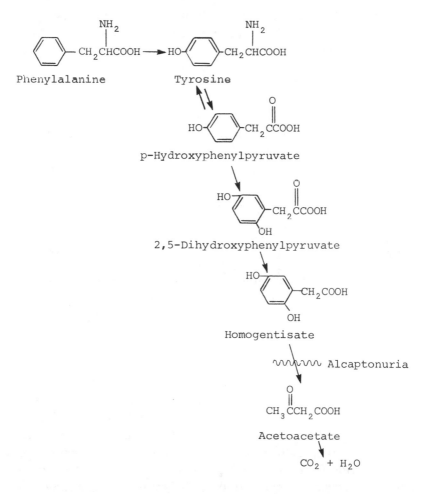

Figure 11.4 – The chemical block in alcaptonuria

Eukaryotic Regulation

 What is the heat shock response?

 Heat shock is a response found in many prokaryotic and eukaryotic cells. When the temperature is raised, the cells stop transcribing the genes that were previously active and instead transcribe a new set of genes called heat shock genes. Translation of the original genes also stops and the heat shock genes are preferentially translated. This event occurs in *Drosophila*, yeast, corn, and cultured mammalian cells. *Drosophila*'s giant salivary gland chromosomes show nine new chromosomal puffs as a result of high temperatures.

How this regulation is achieved is not known. But four heat shock genes have been cloned and sequenced. They have promoter regions and areas of imperfect dyad symmetry upstream from the promoters. These areas are perfect places for regulatory proteins to bind, since many known controlling elements have such symmetry.

 Do histones control gene activity?

 Histones are the proteins that complex with eukaryotic DNA to form chromosomes. Histones are very similar from cell to cell and from organism to organism; therefore, they cannot be responsible for specific gene regulation. However, they do bind to the DNA so they can insulate it from transcription.

As shown in Figure 11.5, histones can repress the transcription of DNA. They can physically block the polymerases and other enzymes from interacting with the DNA. This repression may be overcome by the action of RNA. RNA may hybridize to the non-transcribing (antisense) strand of the DNA, thus freeing the sense strand for transcription. This occurs in a restricted area of the genome; only a few selected genes are open for transcription at any given time.

Thus, histones have a physical role in the regulation of gene expression. They protect the DNA from transcription enzymes until a signal arrives to initiate proper transcription. The specific regulation may be carried out by the other proteins found in chromosomes: the nonhistone proteins.

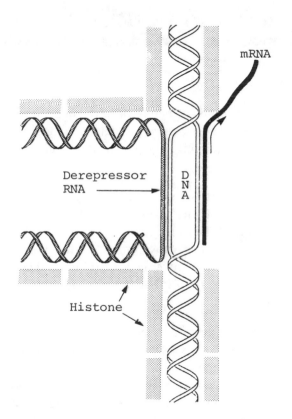

Figure 11.5 — Model for gene repression and selective derepression by histones.

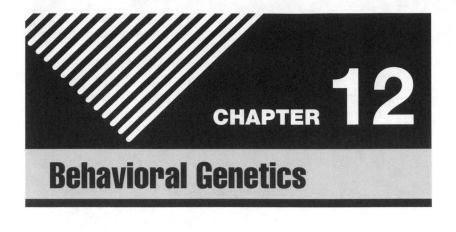

CHAPTER 12

Behavioral Genetics

Many different kinds of behavior have been studied in order to find a genetic basis. These behaviors include mating, geotaxis, barking, hygienic nest cleaning, IQ performance, and schizophrenia, among others.

A genetic basis for behavior can be demonstrated as the result of single genes, single chromosomes, or the genome in general. Single genes affect behavior by causing structural or biochemical changes in the organism. For example, "waltzing" in mice, caused by an autosomal recessive gene, is due to abnormal development of the inner ear. The pattern of inheritance is the same as that for any other autosomal gene.

When trying to determine the number of genes responsible for a particular behavior, crosses between organisms showing variations of the same behavior should be analyzed. Such a cross might be between a basenji (with a high threshold of stimulation for barking) and a cocker spaniel (with a correspondingly low threshold). Use the same techniques discussed in Chapter 6 for determining the number of genes responsible.

A simple genetic model for what appears to be a complex behavior may surface when the behavior is broken down into its components. For example, nest cleaning in honeybees is due to two independent genes: one (*u*) controls uncapping the cell, while the other (*r*) controls removal of the contents.

When looking for a chromosomal basis for behavior, correlations have been made. For example, Down's syndrome (due to trisomy 21) results in mental retardation and Turner's syndrome (one X missing) is associated with perception problems. When looking for a characteristic behavior for XYY males, those in prison populations have generally been studied. However, the behavior should also be evident in higher proportions in XYY males in the general population.

Sometimes a genetic basis for behavior can be demonstrated by examining different strains of the same species. A different strain of *Drosophila* was created by crossing wild-type with yellow flies for seven generations. The wild-type flies from these crosses shared much of the background genotype with the yellow stock. Wild-type flies that were not a product of these crosses would have a different background genotype. Comparisons of behavior can be made and correlated with background genotype.

Where a particular behavior may have an environmental and/or genetic cause, other techniques have been used. For studies of human traits, such as IQ performance, schizophrenia, and epilepsy, twin studies have been used. Since monozygotic twins are genetically more similar than dizygotic twins, a behavioral trait with a genetic component would show higher concordance among the former. In addition, comparisons between twins reared apart and twins reared together would show a high correlation for twins reared apart when the behavioral trait is genetic.

Using biochemical analyses to look for a genetic basis for behavior can be misleading. On the one hand, DNA controls the kinds and amounts of protein synthesized in the body. On the other hand, environmental factors can influence body biochemistry.

Problem Solving Examples:

Insects

 Q A cross between a hygienic nest-cleaning queen bee, *uurr*, and a nonhygienic drone honeybee, *UR*, yields nonhygienic bees, *UuRr*. Would a backcross with a hygienic bee result in any hygienic bees in the F_2 generation?

A American foulbrood is a disease of honeybee larvae caused by the pathogen *Bacillus larvae*. The immediate removal of the dead larvae from the hive is required for the maintenance of a safe, hygienic environment. If the diseased bees are not removed, they remain a source of continuous contamination. The honeybees have two independent genes which control their nest-cleaning activities. One gene, *U*, controls the uncapping of cells and the other, *R*, controls the removal of their contents. Bees of a hygienic colony have the genotype *uurr*.

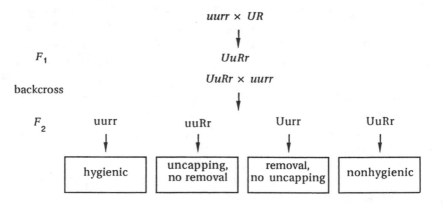

Figure 12.1

The cross of a hygienic queen, *uurr*, and a nonhygienic drone, *UR*, and the backcross are outlined in the diagram shown in Figure 12.1

From this cross, only one of the four offspring would have the genetic ability to both uncap the contaminated cells and remove the dead larvae.

 How is the mating response in houseflies, *Musca domestica*, controlled?

A Female houseflies produce (Z)-9-tricosene, a pheromone that attracts male flies. This pheromone has been named muscalure. The effects of the pheromone on the individual mating responses of different males were studied by using extracts containing the pheromone.

Pseudoflies were made from knotted black shoelaces sprinkled with benzene extracts from female flies which contained the pheromone. Controls were made by sprinkling knotted shoelaces with only the solvent benzene. The quantity and quality of the pheromone, the female flies from which the chemical was extracted, and the light and the temperature were controlled in this study. A total of 347 males were individually observed in their responses.

The results of this experiment showed that two components of behavior are involved in the mating response. These are a pheromone-mediated attraction to the treated pseudoflies and the activity of the individual male flies. The pheromone-mediated attraction is under genetic control since a receptor protein is needed for chemical binding. The activity of the individual males is also under some sort of genetic control. Such characteristics as the number of mating strikes (number of times from flight to mount) are inheritable. Selective breeding from males with the most or fewest mating strikes was performed through the F_4 generation with virgin females. The responsiveness of each generation indicated the inheritance of genes from the parents.

Vertebrates

Q Hybrids between two species of African parrots, *Agapornis roseicollis* and *A. fischeri*, have difficulty in preparing their nests. Why do these lovebirds have such difficulty?

A Each of these lovebird species has its own way of carrying nest-building material. Hybrids try to use both methods simultaneously and hence get confused. It takes the hybrids about three years before they can successfully build nests.

Agapornis roseicollis females carry strips of nesting material (bark, leaves, or paper) tucked between their lower back feathers, Figure 12.2 They can carry several strips at one time. *A. fischeri* females carry the same types of nesting materials in addition to twigs individually in their beaks. Hybrids almost always try to carry the strips of material in their feathers; they are never successful. The hybrid bird awkwardly attempts to tuck the strips in its feathers. It uses the wrong movements and cannot carry any materials to its nest site. The hybrid female can only carry material in her beak, but it takes her three years to successfully learn this. Even then, she is not as adept at carrying strips as an *A. fischeri* female.

Figure 12.2 — Agapornis roseicollis with paper strips tucked between her feathers.

This behavior is controlled polygenically. But further studies of crosses need to be done for a more detailed analysis of the genes that control the nest-building activity of these birds.

 Can an extra Y chromosome (XYY) modify behavior?

 In 1967, a study in a maximum security hospital in Scotland suggested that the antisocial behavior of some of the inmates was due to an XYY chromosome set. W. Price and P. Jacobs compared the crimes and sex chromosomes of a group of men. They concluded from their examination of the men and their lives that the XYY males did not have a family background that was responsible for their wayward behavior. They blamed the men's behavior on their extra Y chromosome.

This conclusion is conveniently reached. D. L. Rimoin and R. N. Schimke, however, indicate that XYY may occur in as many as 1 in 300 live births and that this is more frequent than the incidence of troublesome behavior. A survey in England has not revealed the significantly greater incidence of XYY men in institutions that would be expected in nonrandom distributions.

The extra Y chromosome may predispose a male to a more aggressive attitude. However, with the amount of environmental factors that influence behavior, a genetic basis for man's violent and antisocial behavior is extremely difficult to isolate and identify.

About 0.5 percent of the American population have epilepsy, the falling sickness. Discuss the genetics of this disease.

Epilepsy is a nervous disorder which usually results from injuries to the cerebral cortex. Such damage can be from heredity, infection, or trauma. Some doctors have singled out the hereditary basis of epilepsy as the most important.

Epileptic attacks occur when neurons are discharged in a spontaneous and uncontrolled fashion. When these discharges spread for short distances, the attacks are mild. However, when the discharges spread for long distances, severe seizures containing convulsions and unconsciousness result.

This disease is due to an autosomal recessive trait. One form of epilepsy follows Mendelian inheritance so it is passed from heterozygous parents to their children in a 1:4 ratio. Studies of twins show that the concordance in monozygotic twins is higher than the concordance in dizygotic twins. Thus, the genotype plays a very important part in the acquisition of epilepsy.

 Are there any differences in sensory, perceptual, and motor processes among races?

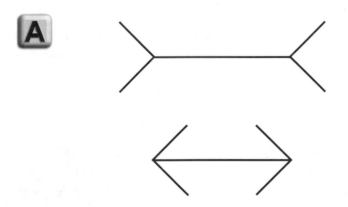

Figure 12.3 — Muller-Lyer illusion. Both horizontal lines are of equal length, yet the top line is frequently distinguished as being longer than the bottom line.

Not many studies have attempted to investigate genetic aspects of sensory and motor processes. The answer to this question is therefore very sketchy.

Late in the 1800's, Native American subjects were found to have the lowest average latency for reaction time to visual, auditory, and tactile stimuli. African-Caucasian hybrids followed and Caucasians were the slowest to react. In a later study, Torres Strait Islanders were found to have greater visual acuity than European groups. Weight discrimination, pain threshold, and olfactory acuity were discussed by Spuhler and Lindzey in 1967. More recent studies have shown that certain optical illusions, such as the Muller-Lyer illusion shown in Figure 12.3, are more common among Americans than among African Bushmen.

At the present, however, there is little compelling evidence, one way or the other, for racial difference or equality in sensory and motor processes.

CHAPTER 13

Immunogenetics

Two types of lymphocytes, B- and T-cells, provide specific immunity against foreign antigens. B-cells produce circulating antibodies which react with antigens. T-cells provide a cell-mediated response to foreign cells. The specificity of the T-cell reaction is based upon the receptor proteins that form on their cell surfaces. We are interested in the genetic controls of antibody production for B-cells and of receptor proteins for T-cells.

To understand the genetics of antibody production, we must first be familiar with its structure. Draw a diagram of the antibody indicating light and heavy chains. Note the variable regions, which provide the antigen-binding site, and the constant regions, which identify the class of antibody and the species it came from.

We need to explain the tremendous variability of antibodies. In understanding the clonal selection theory, we see that exposure to a foreign antigen stimulates cell division of preexisting B-cells that are programmed to make the corresponding antibody. However, we must still explain how the cell genetically controls production of the original B-cells. In evaluating the validity of the three theories of antibody production (germline hypothesis, somatic mutation hypothesis, and recombination hypothesis), you should think about how much of the genome must be devoted to antibody production for each.

Hybridization experiments provide evidence supporting one of these theories of antibody production. An understanding of this technique is important. Remember that mRNA complements the DNA from which it was transcribed. When the two strands of DNA are experimentally separated and mixed with mRNA, the latter forms hydrogen bonds with its complement. We can detect this hybridization by using radioactively labelled mRNA. By using a messenger that codes for a particular antibody, we can locate the corresponding portion(s) of the genome by hybridization.

The variable regions of the light and heavy chains have been found to form by splicing a certain number of DNA sequences together. Each of these DNA sequences exists in variable forms in the genome. Multiply the number of sequences by the number of forms it has to obtain the number of variable regions that can be made for a particular chain.

The genetics of T-cell production are based upon understanding the major histocompatibility complex (MHC). One portion of the MHC codes for the T-cell receptor proteins that recognize foreign antigens. These T-cells can cause skin graft rejection, kill tumor cells, and kill virus-infected cells.

Evidence for a genetic basis for transplant incompatibility, such as skin graft rejection, can be obtained by using inbred strains of animals. Such inbred strains have many homozygous gene loci as the result of breeding siblings for many generations. Different inbred strains can be developed that are homozygous for different alleles. A cross between two different inbred strains will produce offspring heterozygous for many gene loci. We test the effects of different genetic backgrounds for the skin graft by choosing either parent or heterozygous offspring as graft recipients.

In predicting the immune response to a virus-infected cell, you should realize that such a cell will be recognized as foreign by the body.

As part of T-cell production, the body is able to distinguish between self and non-self. Self is defined by a set of proteins found on the surface of most cells in the body. These proteins are coded for by another portion of the MHC. Normally T-cells only form against foreign proteins, but when they form against self, autoimmune disease can result.

Problem Solving Examples:

Basics

Q What is the difference between T-cells and B-cells?

A T-cells and B-cells are activated forms of lymphocytes that result in response to antigens. Morphologically, T- and B-cells are indistinguishable from each other. They arise from the same type of undifferentiated stem cell. Their difference lies in the location in which they differentiate and in their function.

Figure 13.1 shows how a stem cell originating from bone marrow can differentiate into two types of cells. T-cells arise when the stem cells migrate to the thymus. B-cells arise when the stem cells migrate to an intestinal gland, called the bursa, in birds. In mammals, the stem cells develop within the bone marrow and then migrate to peripheral lymphoid tissues to become B cells.

An animal whose thymus has been removed is unable to mount a cell-mediated attack on antigens. Likewise, an animal whose bursa has been removed cannot produce circulating antibodies. T-cells, when activated by an antigen, can produce lymphokines that act in the cell-mediated immune response. When B-cells are activated, they produce antibodies which react with freely circulating antigens in the humoral immune response.

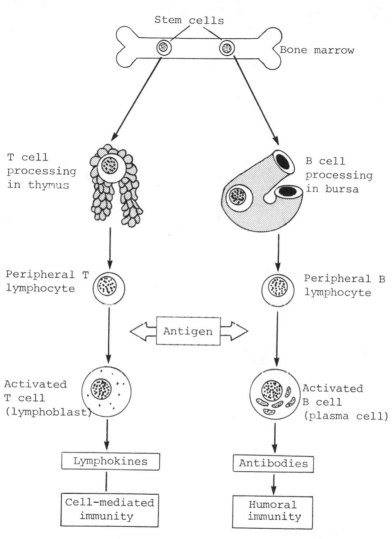

Figure 13.1

Q Any protein can elicit an antibody response. How can an organism make so many specific antibodies?

A

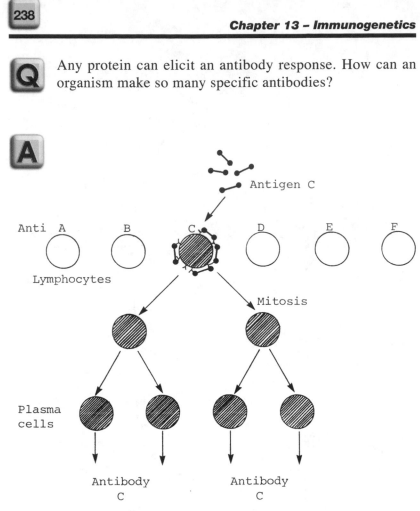

Figure 13.2

The clonal selection theory was proposed in the 1950's by Sir Macfarlane Burnet to explain immunity. His theory states that millions of specific lymphocytes exist in the body. Each secretes an antibody that is specific for a single antigen. When the antigen is introduced to the body, its specific antibody becomes activated. It divides mitotically to form a clone of identical cells (see Figure

13.2). Each of these cells is specific for that antigen. When these lymphocytes are no longer needed, they circulate in a relatively unreactive state throughout the body.

The next time the same antigen is encountered, the cell's immune response is much quicker since the supply of the specific antibody-producing lymphocytes has been greatly increased by the mitotic process. The persistence of these long-lived lymphocytes is the basis for immunological memory.

 Supposing that the clonal selection theory is correct, how can an organism genetically make such diverse proteins?

 There are three theories that account for this diversity. They are the germline hypothesis, the somatic mutation theory, and the rearrangement theory.

The germline hypothesis states that all of the possible sequences arc carried in the DNA. This means that each mammalian genome would need to carry the information to make more than 10^8 anti bodies.

The somatic mutation theory says that the actual number of antibody genes was initially small. The diversity arose through mutation. This implies that the immunoglobulin system is very random.

The rearrangement theory suggests that separated germline sequences come together in all possible combinations via recombination. The variable gene segments can come together in this way to create immense diversity.

To some extent, all of these theories are based on actual mechanisms. These mechanisms, among others, diversify the antibody sequences so that the millions of antigens can be recognized by a single class of protein.

Genes

How are the variable portions of heavy chains combined to create diversity in the antibody sequences?

The variable portions of heavy chains are organized like the variable portions of light chains. The major difference between them is that three separate DNA regions must be combined in heavy chains. These regions are called *V*, *D* (for diversity), and J_H. In heavy chains two joining events, *V–D* and *VD–J*, must occur.

DNA hybridization studies have detected 15 *D* regions. The current estimates for *V* and J_H regions are 250 and 4 respectively. The possible $V–D–J_H$ joining reactions can make $250 \times 15 \times 4 = 15,000$ different variable genes for heavy chains.

Since the sequences for the heavy chains and light chains are on separate chromosomes, recombination between them is rare. This almost ensures that a light chain's variable sequence does not combine with a heavy chain's *J* sequence.

How can the genes for an IgM molecule encode for an IgG molecule with the same specificity later in the immune response?

The five immunoglobulin classes, IgM, IgG, IgD, IgA, and IgE, differ only in the constant regions of their heavy chains. These constant regions are encoded by a cluster of genes on the same chromosome. Class switching is the term used to describe the change from one immunoglobulin class to another.

There are two recombination events that are needed in order for IgG to be produced, see Figure 13.3. The first event attaches a V_H gene to a C_μ gene at one of the *J* segments. This sequence is used to synthesize IgM. The second recombination event attaches $V_H J_H$ to a C_γ gene. The IgG molecule which is synthesized from this sequence has the same variable sequences as the previous immuno-globulin and, hence, the same specificity.

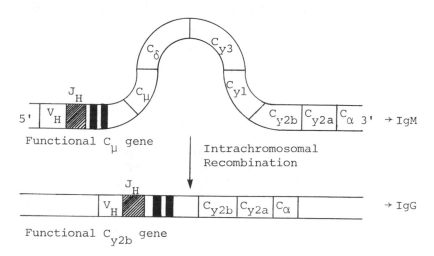

Figure 13.3

Q How can crosses involving strains of highly inbred mice be used to determine a genetic basis for transplant incompatibility?

A Mouse strains that are homozygous at nearly all loci can be obtained by mating brothers and sisters for many generations. Different inbred strains will have different alleles that are homozygous. We can test two such inbred strains for histocompatibility.

Any skin transplant made within a strain is readily and permanently accepted. A transplant between two individuals of different strains does not take. When these strains are crossed and the F_1 generation is tested for hybrid graft rejection, the results are as in Table 13.1. These results show that a graft from either parent or from the hybrid will be accepted when the recipient is a hybrid. The results also show that a graft from the F_1 hybrid will not take on either of the parents, but it will on siblings.

This experiment suggests that transplant rejection (or acceptance) has a genetic basis. It also suggests that codominant alleles are involved because the progeny exhibit antigenic properties of both of the parents.

Table 13.1

	Recipient		
Donor	Male Parent Strain	Female Parent Strain	Progeny
Male parent strain	+(1)	–(2)	+(3)
Female parent strain	–(2)	+(1)	+(3)
Progeny	–(4)	–(4)	+(3)

(1) grafts within a strain

(2) grafts between strains

(3) grafts from parents or siblings

(4) grafts from progeny

Note: + indicates a successful graft, – indicates a rejected graft.

CHAPTER 14

Retroviruses

Retrovirus research over the past eight decades has greatly contributed to our knowledge of cancer, the cell cycle, signal transduction, gene expression, genetics, and immunology. However, it was only the relatively recent implication of the human immunodeficiency virus (HIV) as the causative agent of the Acquired Immunodeficiency Syndrome (AIDS) that hurled them into the spotlight of public attention.

In the decades since the first reports of AIDS and HIV, the spread of HIV in the United States alone reached epidemic proportions. New US AIDS cases reached a peak in 1993, with 78,954 new cases reported that year. Thanks to an immense media campaign, most people now know about HIV and its modes of transmission, so that its incidence is plateauing. People are also being taught that HIV works by dismantling a critical leg of the immune system, the T-helper cells. Unfortunately, despite our increasing understanding of how the virus operates, no cure or vaccine is yet available for HIV.

Retroviruses were discovered in 1911 by Peyton Rous, who noticed that a "filterable agent" from certain chicken tumors could cause rapid tumor formation when injected into healthy young chickens. Further work revealed several other RNA viruses, from both birds and mammals, with similar tumor-inducing capabilities. These viruses, termed RNA tumor viruses, carry cancer-causing genes called oncogenes, which are of cellular origin. Often these oncogenes are mutated versions of the cellular equivalents (protooncogenes) with consequently altered functions. The majority of known oncogenes were discovered in retroviruses (of which over 50 are known). Research on the retroviral oncogenes and cellular protooncogenes has greatly enhanced our understanding of cancer, gene expression, signal transduction, and even the cell cycle.

In the early 1960's, Howard Temin discovered that RNA tumor viruses replicate through a DNA intermediate, implying that they must make a DNA copy of their RNA genome as part of their life cycle. This finding contradicted the central dogma of molecular biology, which states that genetic information passes only from DNA to RNA to protein. Opposition to Temin's hypothesis was so fierce that few scientists believed him until he and David Baltimore, working independently, isolated reverse transcriptase, the RNA-dependent DNA polymerase.

Retrovirus research has immensely affected biotechnology also. In addition to its biological interest, reverse transcriptase now occupies a central role in recombinant DNA technology. Retroviral vectors are widely used to transfer genes from one cell to another. In fact, they were used in the first recently-initiated gene therapy experiments.

Exciting retrovirus research is continuing today. Recently, immunologists have discovered that some retroviruses encode "superantigens," antigens that interact with not one, but entire subsets of T-cell receptors. *In vivo* this results in deletion of these receptors. It was recently suggested that HIV may encode a superantigen. If true, this finding would be an inroad to understanding how HIV depletes the T-helper cell reservoir and perhaps how to design a vaccine or cure.

Problem Solving Examples:

Retroviruses

 Retroviruses are also divided into three official taxonomic groups, assignments into which are purely functional. Name the three taxonomic divisions and the characteristics of each. To which group or groups do the human pathogens belong?

The three taxons into which retroviruses are grouped are: *Oncoviridae*, whose members induce tumors; *Lentiviridae*, whose members cause slow disease, and *Spumiviridae*, a largely unknown class whose members cause foamy vacuoles in infected cells. The known human retroviruses are the human T-cell leukemia viruses (HTLV-1, HTLV-2) and the human immunodeficiency viruses (HIV-1, HIV-2). All belong to the lentiviruses.

In very basic terms describe the structure of a retroviral virion.

The virion is composed of the RNA genome, a surrounding protein capsid, and an outer lipid bilayer envelope. The RNA genome consists of two identical mRNA-like RNA molecules joined near their 5' ends. A tRNA molecule specific for each type of RNA is hybridized at this same site to each RNA molecule. Tightly associated with the RNA are about two thousand copies of a low molecular weight, basic protein. Another protein forms a structure called a capsid around the coated RNAs. This whole structure is called a nucleocapsid. The nucleocapsid can be of either helical or icosahedral symmetry, depending on the virus in question. Surrounding the nucleocapsid is a host-cell, membrane-derived lipid bilayer known as the envelope. The region between the nucleocapsid and the envelope is the matrix. The viral enzymes reverse transcriptase, protease, and integrase are found here. Two viral proteins are found associated with the envelope. One is a transmembrane protein (*TM*) and the other is a surface, outer-envelope glycoprotein linked to the virion via disulfide bonds with *TM*. This surface protein (*SU*) predictably determines the virus' host range. The enveloped particle is of icosahedral symmetry.

Q The discovery of one aspect of retroviral replication fundamentally shook the field of genetics. What was that discovery? What core belief of molecular genetics did it invalidate?

A In 1964, Howard M. Temin discovered that retroviruses, which are RNA viruses, replicate through a DNA intermediate. This meant that the DNA intermediate (i.e., the provirus) had to be copied from an RNA molecule. This was in direct violation of the central dogma of molecular biology which states that genetic information invariably passes from DNA to RNA to protein. Dr. Temin's discovery was initially met with disbelief and led to a fervent controversy. In the end Temin was proven correct when he and David Baltimore each independently isolated reverse transcriptase. Temin and Baltimore shared the 1975 Nobel Prize in medicine for their work in this area.

Q Over the past two decades retroviruses have profoundly impacted the growing field of molecular biology. What retroviral enzyme has most revolutionized this field?

A Once again the answer is reverse transcriptase, the heretical polymerase that synthesizes DNA from an RNA template. With the aid of this enzyme, mRNA can be copied into complementary DNA (cDNA), allowing for the cloning of all the genes expressed within a tissue and in proportion to their copy number. Furthermore, only the coding region is copied, because the introns are spliced out of mRNA, making it easy to discern the sequence of the encoded protein. The significance of being able to make DNA copies of mRNA is impossible to overstate. All cDNA libraries, virtually all recombinantly expressed proteins, and almost all cloned mammalian genes are the direct result of reverse-transcribing RNA into DNA.

Q All linear genomes share a common problem of replication. Define the problem and describe how the process of reverse transcription elegantly solves it.

A The problem faced by all linear genomes is replicating the entire genome without loss of information from the ends. Recall that no known DNA polymerases can initiate synthesis from a bare template; they can only extend a primer. Furthermore, in all observed cases, this primer is RNA, not DNA. Because all known naturally occurring nucleic acid synthesis proceeds 5' to 3', this loss of information would be from the 5' end(s) of the molecule(s). What primes the addition of nucleotides to the extreme 5' end of each strand?

Retroviruses solved this problem simply by copying the 5' end before copying the rest of the strand. Minus-strand strong-stop DNA is the extreme 5' end of the downstream LTR (i.e., the 5' end of the minus strand). Plus-strand strong-stop DNA is the 5' end of the other strand.

Q Retroviruses are categorized in terms of host range. Define *ecotropic, amphitropic,* and *xenotropic.* What are interference groups?

A Ecotropic retroviruses infect only cells of the species producing the virus. Amphitropic retroviruses can infect several species including the one currently producing the virus. Xenotropic viruses infect species other than the one producing the virus. The latter is a rather confusing concept and is largely a laboratory phenomenon. A researcher can artificially introduce the retrovirus' genetic material into a cell type that it normally does not infect. This host cell produces progeny virus which cannot reinfect it or other cells from the same species.

Researchers categorize retroviruses by their host range. All retroviruses that enter their host cell via the same receptor belong to the same interference group. The name "interference group" comes from an early observation that cells infected with one type of retrovirus resist infection by certain other types of retroviruses. Retrovirologists later learned that these viruses all used the same receptor on the host cell. The viral envelope protein produced by the infected cell mediates this interference. Some of the envelope protein escapes from the membrane and binds to the receptor. The occupied receptor is unavailable for binding of free virus. It should be clear that members of an interference group also belong to the same host range group. However, the reverse is not true. There are typically more than one interference group per host range category.

 You discover a mouse immune to infection by a certain type of retrovirus normally pathogenic towards that strain. Further study reveals that the retrovirus does not enter the cells of this mouse. What is the most likely explanation for your observation? Would you expect other retroviruses of the same interference group to be able to infect this mouse? Why or why not?

Most likely the mouse has a mutation in the receptor for the virus. The mutation would not be a deletion, because the actual function of most retroviral receptors is essential for cell viability. Rather, the mutation probably changes the tertiary structure of the protein slightly so the virus can no longer bind to it. You should realize that both copies of the gene must be mutated—although one could be a knock-out mutation. If only one locus was mutated, the virus could enter the cell via the protein encoded by the remaining locus. You would expect that other members of the same interference group would not be able to infect this mouse either. Recall that all members of an interference group recognize the same receptor protein.

The same researcher now microinjects increasing copies of a cDNA of the vRNA (a dsDNA copy of the vRNA not a provirus) into cells. Predict the results of this experiment using the above question as a format. If you predict the results of the two experiments to differ greatly, explain why.

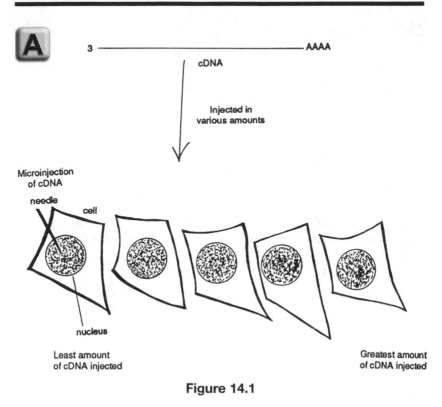

A

3 ——————————————————— AAAA

cDNA

Injected in
various amounts

Microinjection
of cDNA

needle   cell

nucleus

Least amount   Greatest amount
of cDNA injected   of cDNA injected

Figure 14.1

This time the answer is no, progeny virus will not be produced. The main reason a cDNA will not work is that it has no promoter (no U3 from the left LTR, only R and U5) to drive transcription. Hence, no RNA for translating viral proteins or for progeny genomes will be produced. The cDNA cannot be translated or encapsidated.

Q Transcription from the HIV LTR largely depends on the presence of the transcription factor NF-KB, which is activated upon stimulation of the host T-cell. The level of transcription is intially very low but quickly increases to maximal levels. Only after the level of transcription reaches its maximum do *gag, pol,* and *env* proteins appear. Explain the HIV regulatory network responsible for this observation.

A   The rapid increase in transcription level results from a *tat*-mediated positive feedback loop. A positive feedback loop is a process which promotes itself. The initially expressed, multiply spliced mRNA encodes *tat, rev,* and *nef*. As more and more *tat* is made, more and more is available to bind the nascent HIV transcripts, further stimulating transcription and consequently increasing the amount of *tat*. Hence production of *tat* stimulates increased production of *tat*. The increase in transcription increases until increased *tat* levels cannot stimulate the rate of transcription any higher.

As *tat* becomes more abundant so does *rev*. Hence, an increasing number of nascent transcripts can be bound and shepherded to the cytoplasm without undergoing extensive splicing. Sufficient *rev* accumulation occurs shortly after transcription reaches its maximum. This allows for the delay of late gene product expression until transcription levels are very high. (See figure on following page.)

Q   Some HIV isolates differ in their ability to infect various alternative hosts. You learn that these strains differ genetically at one or more clusters in the genome. One of these regions of variability is far more prominent than others. What would you expect to be located at that part of the genome? Why?

A   You would expect that the major class of these mutations would lie in the *env* gene, which in fact they do. Specifically, you would expect them to fall in that part of the gene that encodes the *SU* protein, gp120. The observed mutations do fall in this region, but somewhat surprisingly, they do not seem to fall in the exact same region believed to interact with CD4. Rather, they occur in a region next to the CD4-binding domain. This finding gives credence to the notion that HIV recognizes more than one receptor.

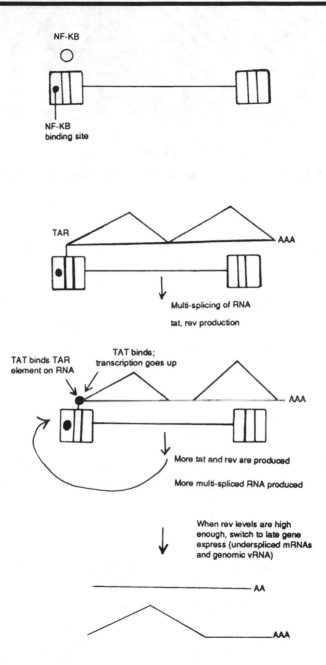

Figure 14.2

CHAPTER 15

Genetic Engineering

Understanding the way in which genetic engineering works depends upon a knowledge of a number of techniques. These include the use of DNA and RNA sequencing, reverse transcriptase, plasmid and virus vectors, and selective media.

Various nucleases, called restriction enzymes, recognize and cut specific DNA sequences. The recognition sites may vary from four to six bases, may be present in some organisms and not others, and may contain palindromes (sequences that read the same in both directions). The cuts may be blunt or staggered. The latter produces sticky ends that are very useful when inserting DNA fragments into plasmids in preparation for molecular cloning.

Restriction maps can be made by radioactively labelling the 3' end of the DNA, treating with specific restriction enzymes, and determining the size of the labelled piece by the distance it moves in gel electrophoresis. This gives us a map of restriction sites, but not the actual DNA sequence.

To understand how Maxam and Gilbert sequenced DNA using gel electrophoresis, you have to know the following:

1. The 5' end of DNA can be identified if radioactively labelled with ^{32}P.

2. The weak hydrogen bonds holding DNA together can be broken, giving two single strands. The strand containing more purines

is the heavy strand. (Remember that purines are double-ring structures and pyrimidines are single-ring structures.) Analysis of only one strand is enough, since the strands are complementary.

3. Different chemicals can be used to cause breaks at different sites in the DNA: guanine, adenine, both cytosine and thymine, and cytosine. Varying fragment lengths result, since the chemicals do not cleave all possible sites in each sample.

4. Varying fragment lengths can be separated by gel electrophoresis, the smallest, and, therefore, the lightest, moving the farthest.

5. The position in the gel tells us the length of the fragment. Therefore, we know the position of the particular base as measured from the 5' end. By reading the bands produced in each of the four gels (one for each chemical), we can determine the base sequence. To determine the position of thymine we must look at the gel that shows cleavage of both cytosine and thymine and compare it with the one for cytosine (there is no chemical that cleaves only thymine).

RNA nucleases aid in RNA sequencing by cleaving specific sites. For example, pancreatic RNase breaks RNA after a pyrimidine. Thus, we know that each fragment produced must end in cytosine or thymine. Further treatment of the fragments cuts the sugar-phosphate backbone after the 3' phosphate when travelling in a 5' ⟶ 3' direction. The first base (at the 5' end) can be recognized because it will have both 5' and 3' phosphates. The last base (at the 3' end) can be recognized because it will have neither. Using this information, we can put the bases within each fragment, and the fragments themselves, in order.

A number of techniques exist for manufacturing a DNA sequence, either based upon a known protein structure or by copying mRNA using reverse transcriptase. Thus, it is possible to make the gene for a protein, such as insulin. Bacteria with such genes inserted can divide and produce large quantities of the protein, a process called **molecular cloning**.

To figure out how this is possible, think about how genetic material can be transferred into bacterial cells. Keep in mind that bacteria can undergo conjugation, transformation, and transduction. Then the use of plasmid vectors or viruses and the use of calcium for greater permeability will make sense.

Also, remember that if we are to use the host cells to clone DNA, we must insert it into its genome. Think about how restriction enzymes as well as ligases might make this possible.

For this DNA transfer, we would also want to separate out the cells that successfully incorporate it. If this DNA has a nutritional or antibiotic resistant marker on it, imagine how selective media might help.

The same general approach to genetic engineering can be applied to mammalian cells or cells of diploid organisms. When assessing the possible impact of gene transfer on the recipient, include the role of regulatory genes and the presence of introns in eukaryotic genomes.

Problem Solving Examples:

Methods

 What is a plasmid vector?

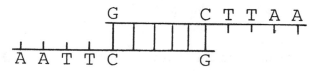

Figure 15.1 — Sticky ends of a piece of DNA cut with the restriction enzyme EcoRI.

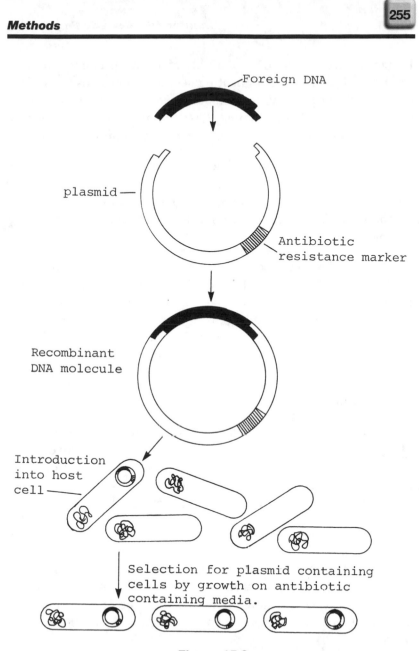

Figure 15.2

Plasmids are extrachromosomal, circular pieces of bacterial DNA. They are self-replicating accessory chromosomes. They carry genes for antibiotic resistance, metabolism of natural products, and production of toxins. Plasmids have become important components in the manipulation of genes in cloning experiments.

When the restriction enzyme *EcoR*I is used to cut a piece of DNA, it leaves "sticky" ends, Figure 15.1. Such a fragment can be inserted into a circular plasmid DNA that has been similarly treated. As shown in Figure 15.2, these hybrid plasmids can be used to infect bacteria.

A plasmid can be used as a means of introducing a foreign piece of DNA into a bacterial cell. Since the plasmid is self-replicating, the foreign DNA will remain a part of the plasmid and a part of the bacterial strain as long as the plasmid stays in a cell. Thus, clones of cells containing a piece of foreign DNA can be produced. This is the basis of the recombinant DNA industry.

 How has the action of reverse transcriptase been exploited by biologists?

In 1970, Howard Temin and David Baltimore independently discovered reverse transcriptase. Since its discovery, this viral enzyme has been used in many ways by research biologists. Its unique ability to catalyze the synthesis of DNA from RNA has established it as an important tool in genetic research.

Reverse transcriptase is coded for by the nucleic acid of retroviruses. When retroviruses infect a bacterial host, their RNA genomes are transcribed into DNA by reverse transcriptase which is present in small amounts in the viral protein coat. Once in the DNA form, the viral genome integrates into the host chromosome as a provirus. The provirus is then replicated as a part of the bacterial genome.

The mechanism of this enzyme is similar to that of other DNA polymerases. The DNA is synthesized in the 5' to 3' direction. It needs a primer to begin this synthesis. The primer is a noncovalently bound tRNA that was picked up from the host during the previous round of infection. The DNA chain can be added to the 3' end of this tRNA molecule. Somehow, double-stranded circular DNA molecules are made from this single-stranded DNA copy. These circular proviruses are now ready for insertion into the host genome.

This enzyme has proven to be a useful tool to the molecular biologist. It can be used to make DNA copies of any RNA that can be purified. This function can be useful in many types of experiments. Purified mRNA can be obtained from cells that are specialized to make specific proteins (e.g., hemoglobin from red blood cells and insulin from mammalian pancreas cells). The DNA copy of mRNAs from these cells can be used to find the sequence in the cells' own DNA. Thus, a specific area of the mass of DNA can be focused on. In similar ways, split genes and differences between hnRNA and mRNA can be studied. But perhaps most importantly, reverse transcriptase is a necessary reagent for genetic engineering with recombinant DNA. The complementary DNA (cDNA) that is transcribed from an mRNA is what is inserted into plasmids to create recombinant DNA molecules. Thus, this enzyme is a very significant part of the blossoming genetic technology.

Q What is a retroviral vector? What discovery demonstrated that retroviruses might be commandeered to transfer genes from one cell to another? What is a helper cell (also called a packaging cell)? What sequences must a retroviral vector possess in order to be functional?

A Retroviral vectors are essentially retroviruses engineered to carry genes chosen by a researcher "in place" of their own genes. The discovery that certain highly oncogenic, replication-defective retroviruses transduce cellularly derived genes (oncogenes) gave the first inclinations that retroviruses could be commandeered as gene transfer vehicles. The finding that the transducing virus could be packaged if its deleted proteins were supplied in trans by a coinfecting nontransducing wild-type virus (a helper virus) led to the idea that cell lines could be established to express all the virus proteins for the purpose of passaging the vector. Such cells, termed helper or packaging cells, supply all virus proteins but produce no replication-competent virus. The vector must possess the encap-sidation sequences, PBS, PPT, U3 attachment site, U5, and R. It must also have either U3 or a promoter to generate full-length genomic transcripts. However, U3 itself is not necessary; any promoter will do.

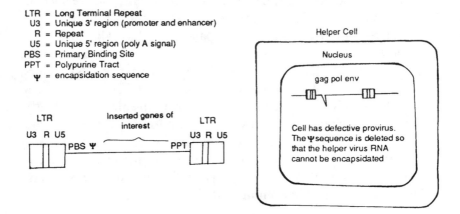

LTR = Long Terminal Repeat
U3 = Unique 3' region (promoter and enhancer)
R = Repeat
U5 = Unique 5' region (poly A signal)
PBS = Primary Binding Site
PPT = Polypurine Tract
Ψ = encapsidation sequence

Helper Cell

Nucleus

gag pol env

Cell has defective provirus. The Ψ sequence is deleted so that the helper virus RNA cannot be encapsidated

LTR   Inserted genes of interest   LTR
U3 R U5   U3 R U5
PBS Ψ   PPT

Figure 15.3

Q What is a shuttle vector?

A Shuttle vectors contain sequences that signal DNA replication in *E. coli* and sequences that signal replication in yeast. Thus, the plasmid can be shuttled back and forth between yeast and *E. coli* and be replicated in both organisms. Shuttle vectors can be used to clone many genes. Total genomic yeast DNA is cut with a restriction enzyme. The fragments are inserted into shuttle vectors using recombinant DNA techniques. These plasmids are propagated in *E. coli*. This mixed population of plasmids is introduced into mutant yeast spheroplasts. Any recombinant that complements the mutation in yeast can be identified and reintroduced into *E. coli*. Once in *E. coli*, it can be grown in large amounts and studied further. Theoretically, any gene for which a mutation can be identified can be cloned this way.

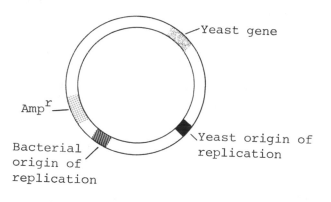

Figure 15.4

What are the possible hazards of molecular cloning?

 As with all new technologies, cloning has possible hazards. Virulent strains of the ubiquitous *E. coli* could spread disease throughout human populations if experiments introducing viral genes into the bacterial genome were performed carelessly. Most scientists in the early days of cloning, the 1970's, were concerned about the potential military applications of virulent bacteria as part of biological warfare. Another potential hazard surfaced in 1972. The fear was about the finding that the DNA of mice, and possibly all higher cells, harbored latent RNA tumor virus genes. There was then the possibility of introducing cancer-causing genes into human cells in the search for antibody genes.

In 1975 in California, the Asilomar Conference proposed guidelines for recombinant DNA research. Among the guidelines were rules for the safe handling of recombinants. The development of "safe" bacterial hosts and vectors was demanded. The first "safe" bacterium was the *E. coli* strain $K12$ named []χ1776. This strain cannot live without diaminopimelic acid in its environment. This compound is not present in human intestines, so the bacterium would be unable to survive in human hosts. This bacterium also has a fragile cell wall that lyses in low salt concentrations or in traces of detergent. However, the introduction of recombinant DNA molecules was difficult in this strain. Other "safe" bacteria have since been developed that greatly lessen the risk of an accidental spread of disease.

Applications

 How can genetic engineering be used to improve agricultural crops?

 Agriculture has been using the principles of Mendelian genetics for thousands of years. The yields of wheat and corn have steadily increased over the past 50 years by the use of close inbreeding and rigorous artificial selection. This produces distinct and genetically uniform varieties with both desired and undesired traits. These varieties have improved crop yields and introduced hybrid vigor. For instance, genes were introduced, by sexual crosses, from a semi-dwarf variety of Japanese wheat to a Mexican wheat strain. The hybrid had greater wind resistance and needed less growth before flowering because the straw was shorter and stiffer; this meant greater adaptability to the region and greater disease and insect resistance.

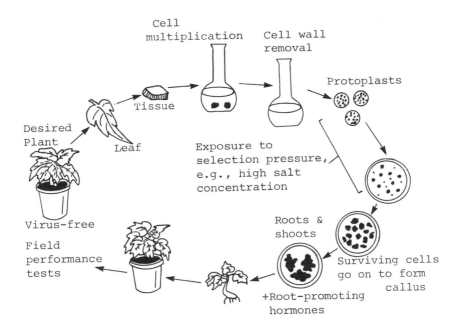

Figure 15.5 — The process of plant propagation from single cells in culture can produce plants with selected characteristics. These selections must be tested in the field to evaluate their performance.

The recent discovery of the crown gall plasmid system has created the possibility for recombinant DNA techniques to be applied to plants. This would be much faster than conventional breeding and would enable the introduction of genes from one sexually incompatible species to another. However, the isolation of specific genes that affect crop yield is extremely difficult.

Thus, plant breeders have been using genetics for a long time. The techniques of recombinant DNA may eventually be used to improve agricultural crops with greater specificity and speed than is available in the traditional methods.

CHAPTER 16

Probabilities and Statistics

A number of statistical procedures are useful for genetics. They are listed below with explanations. As you use these procedures you will notice that the total number of organisms is frequently incorporated. Remember that as sample size becomes smaller, the effects of random variations become greater. Conclusions based upon smaller sample size must be made cautiously.

The mean, median, and mode describe centrally occurring values in a sample. The **mean** is the average value in a sample:

$$x = \frac{\Sigma x}{n}$$

$\bar{x}$ = mean of sample

Σx = sum of all quantities in sample

n = number in sample

The **median** is the central or middle value. Where the number in the sample is even, the two middle values are averaged. The mode is the most frequently occurring value.

The dispersion or amount of variation of the sample is expressed as the variance, standard deviation, standard error of the mean, mean deviation about the median, and the coefficient of variation. **Variance** (s^2) is defined as:

$$s^2 = \frac{\Sigma(x_i - \bar{x})^2}{n-1}$$

x_i = measurement for each member of sample.

The **standard deviation** (s) equals the square root of the variance.

$$s = \sqrt{s^2} = \sqrt{\frac{\Sigma(x_i - \bar{x})^2}{n-1}}$$

The **standard error of the mean** *(S. E.)* is defined as:

$$S.E. = \frac{s}{\sqrt{n}}$$

The **mean deviation about the median**

$$= \frac{\Sigma|\bar{x} - N|}{N}$$

where N equals the median.

For the **coefficient of variation** (V),

$$V = \frac{s}{x}$$

We can determine whether two samples are statistically different by using the **standard error of the difference of the means** *(S.E.$_D$)*.

$$S.E._D = (S.E._A)^2 + (S.E._B)^2$$

where A and B are the two samples. The difference between the means of the two samples must be divided by the standard error of the difference in the means to obtain a ratio (t). Using a t values chart and allowing for a probability of 0.05, any t value higher than indicated in the chart indicates statistical significance.

We can express the contribution of environment and genes to the variation of a quantitative trait as **phenotypic variance** (V_P).

$$V_P = V_G + V_E + V_{GE}$$

$$V_G = V_A + V_D + V_I$$

V_G = genetic variance

V_A = genetic variance due to additive genes

V_D = genetic variance due to dominant genes

V_I = genetic variance due to epistasis

V_E = environmental variance

V_{GE} = variance due to genetic and environmental interactions

A measure of inheritance or **heritability** (H) is given as the ratio of additive genetic variance to phenotypic variance. Narrow variance is given by the formula:

$$h^2 = \frac{V_A}{V_P}$$

When $h^2 = 1$, there is no environmental influence. When $h^2 = 0$, there is no genetic basis. Broad variance is expressed by

$$h^2 = \frac{V_G}{V_P}$$

Genetics is based upon the rules of **probability**. The probability of an event occurring is

$$\frac{\text{the number of times that a particular event will occur}}{\text{the number of total trials}}.$$

The probability of two independent events occurring at the same time is the product of their probabilities. In determining such a

probability you may have to work out the probability for each event first. This could include determining the genotypes of parents and the probability of certain gametes forming. Remember that the probability of reoccurrence in subsequent children has nothing to do with previous offspring, since they are forming from a large gamete pool.

One application of probability is the *Hardy-Weinberg Law,* a powerful tool for studying populations.

The **binomial distribution** also provides an application for probabilities. For situations where two independent outcomes are possible for each of many trials, the probability of one occurrence $(P)(X)$ is:

$$P(X) = \frac{N!}{X!(N-X)!} p^x q^{n-x}$$

N = total number of trials

X = number of one type of occurrence

$N - X$ = number of other type of occurrence

p = probability of first type of occurrence in a single trial

q = probability of second type of occurrence in a single trial

This formula might be used to determine the probability of a certain combination of males and females or of two different phenotypes, given a particular family size.

For a normal distribution we can determine the probability that the variable will fall within a particular range using the **Z-score**.

$$\text{Z-score} = \frac{x - \text{mean}}{\text{standard deviation}}$$

x = normal random variable

Given the Z-score, its probabilities can be found on a chart.

The **chi-square test** (χ^2) is a way of determining whether observed data fits the hypothesis. The hypothesis might be stated as a ratio, but should be converted to actual numbers for use in the chi square. Let the observed total equal the expected total. Multiply the probability of each by the expected total. Multiply the probability of each by the expected total to get the expected number for each class. The following formula is used to calculate a chi square value:

$\chi^2 = (d^2/e)$

d = observed – expected

e = expected

To find the probability of obtaining the observed values by chance alone (assuming the hypothesis is correct), a chi square table must be used. First, the degrees of freedom (df) must be determined.

$df = n - i$

where n = number of classes

The chi square value is found on the chart for the calculated degrees of freedom and the probability is read from the top of the table. If the probability equals or is greater than 0.05, then the hypothesis is accepted.

Problem Solving Examples:

General Probability and Applications

 A deck of playing cards is thoroughly shuffled and a card is drawn from the deck. What is the probability that the card drawn is the ace of diamonds?

The probability of an event occurring is

$$\frac{\text{the number of ways the event can occur}}{\text{the number of possible outcomes}}.$$

In our case there is one way the event can occur, for there is only one ace of diamonds and there are 52 possible outcomes (for there are 52 cards in the deck). Hence the probability that the card drawn is the ace of diamonds is 1/52.

   What is the probability of getting a 5 on each of two successive rolls of a balanced die?

We are dealing with separate rolls of a balanced die. The 2 rolls are independent; therefore, we invoke the following multiplication rule: The probability of getting any particular combination in two or more independent trials will be the product of their individual probabilities. The probability of getting a 5 on any single toss is 1/6 and by the multiplication rule

$$P(5 \text{ and } 5) \ = \frac{1}{6} \times \frac{1}{6} = \frac{1}{36}$$

Note also that the problem could have been stated as follows:

What is the probability of rolling 2 balanced dice simultaneously and getting a 5 on each?

   Consider that in humans red-green colorblindness is controlled by a recessive X-linked gene, *c*. Assume that a normal-visioned woman, whose father was colorblind, marries a normal-visioned man.

What is the probability that their first child will be colorblind?

Since this trait is sex-linked, we first must consider whether sex of the child is important, and determine the genotypes of the parents. The woman has to be heterozygous, *Cc*, since her father was colorblind, and the man must be $C\nearrow$ since he was normal-visioned. As a consequence, the only children that can exhibit the trait will be sons. Therefore, the probability of the first child being colorblind means that the child must also be a male.

Thus,

$$P = P(\text{male}) \times P(\text{colorblind}) = \frac{1}{2} \times \frac{1}{2} = \frac{1}{4}$$

Q Consider the following three traits in the fruit fly, *Drosophila melanogaster,* each controlled by a single pair of contrasting genes exhibiting complete dominance:

wing length	body color	eye color
long wings = L	gray body = B	dull red dyes = R
short wings = l	black body = b	brown eyes = r

Assume that each pair of genes is located in a different pair of chromosomes (i.e., independent gene pairs). In a cross between two flies heterozygous for each pair of genes, what is the probability that the first adult fly emerging is short-winged, gray-bodied, and red-eyed?

A Since the three traits are controlled by independent gene pairs, we can use the *Probability Law for Independent Events,* which states that the probability of simultaneous occurrence of independent events is equal to the product of their separate probabilities.

The probability of getting short wings from this cross is 1/4, the probability of getting gray body is 3/4, and the probability of getting red eyes is 3/4. Thus,

$$P = P(\text{short}) \times P(\text{gray}) \times P(\text{red}) = (1/4)(3/4)(3/4) = 9/64.$$

Conditional Probability

 Find the probability of throwing at least one of the following totals on a single throw of a pair of dice: a total of 5, a total of 6, or a total of 7.

Define the events *A, B,* and *C* as follows:

Event *A*: a total of 5 is thrown,
Event *B:* a total of 6 is thrown,
Event *C:* a total of 7 is thrown.

 Only one of these three events can occur at one time. The occurrence of any one excludes the occurrence of any of the others. Such events are called mutually exclusive.

Let $A \cup B \cup C$ = the event that at least a 5, 6, or 7 is thrown.

$$P(A \cup B \cup C) = P(A) + P(B) + P(C)$$

because the events are mutually exclusive.

Referring to a previous problem we see that

$$P(A) = \frac{4}{36}, \ P(B) = \frac{5}{36}, \text{ and } P(C) = \frac{6}{36},$$

Therefore,

$$P(A \cup B \cup C) = \frac{4}{36} + \frac{5}{36} + \frac{6}{36} = \frac{15}{36} = \frac{5}{12}$$

Normal Distribution

 Distinguish between *a* discrete variable and a continuous variable and give examples of each.

A discrete random variable is a variable which can take on only isolated values.

Some examples of discrete variables are:

(1) the number of offspring in a mouse litter;

(2) the number of girls in families with 4 children;

(3) the number of apples in a bushel;

(4) the number of sparrows per acre of land.

Each of these examples are counts. Many situations do not involve counting, but rather, measurement. In this case we could say that a boy is 65 inches tall or if measured more accurately 65.3 inches, or even more accurately 65.32 inches. In other words, a person's height may be a range of values, and not just isolated values such as 64, 65, 66 inches.

Some examples of continuous variables are:

(1) the time it takes for an electric component to fail;

(2) the cruising speeds of various airplanes;

(3) the heights of a hybrid strain of plants;

(4) the length of people's toes.

 If a random variable X is normally distributed with a mean of 118 and a standard deviation of 11, what Z-scores correspond to raw scores of 115, 134, and 99?

 To convert a raw score to a Z-score we subtract the mean and divide by the standard deviation. Thus,

$$\text{Z-score} = \frac{\text{raw score} - \text{mean}}{\text{standard deviation}}.$$

Thus,

$$\frac{115-118}{11} = \frac{-3}{11} = -0.27;$$

a Z-score of –0.27 corresponds to a raw score of 115.

$$Z = \frac{134-118}{11} = \frac{16}{11} = 1.45$$

or a Z-score of 1.45 corresponds to a raw score of 134. And

$$Z = \frac{99-118}{11} = -1.73,$$

or a Z-score of –1.73 corresponds to a raw score of 99.

 Find $Pr(-0.47 < z < 0.94)$.

$Pr(-0.47 \leq z \leq 0.94)$ is equal to the shaded area in Figure 1. To find the value of the shaded area we add the areas labelled $A(-0.47)$ and $A(0.94)$.

$$Pr(-0.47 \leq z \leq 0.94) = A(-0.47) + A(0.94)$$

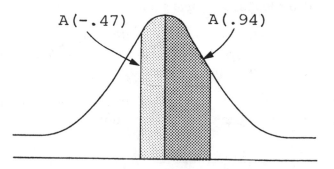

Figure 16.1

By the symmetry of the normal distribution, $A(-0.47) = A(0.47)$ = 0.18082 from the table on page 275.

Also, $A(0.94) = 0.32639$, so

$Pr(-0.47 < Z < 0.94) = 0.18082 + 0.32639 = 0.50721.$

 If X has a normal distribution with mean 9 and standard deviation 3, find $P(5 < X < 11)$.

 First, we convert our X-scores to Z-scores by subtracting the mean and dividing by the standard deviation. Next, we consult tables for the standard normal distribution found on page 275.

Thus,

$$P(5 < X < 1) = P\left[\frac{5-9}{3} < \frac{X-9}{3} < \frac{11-9}{3}\right]$$
$$= P\left[\frac{-4}{3} < Z < \frac{2}{3}\right]$$
$$= \Phi(0.66) - \Phi(-0.133)$$
$$= 0.74537 - 0.09176 = 0.65361$$

 Miniature poodles are thought to have a mean height of 12 inches and a standard deviation of 1.8 inches. If height is measured to the nearest inch, find the percentage of poodles having a height exceeding 14 inches.

 Let X be the height of a randomly selected poodle. X has mean 12 and standard deviation 1.8. Because the heights are measured to the nearest inch, any height that is greater than 13.5 or less than 14.5 is recorded as 14.

To find the percentage of poodles such that height, X, is greater than 14, we must find the percentage of poodles whose heights are greater than 13.5.

$Pr(X \geq 13.5)$ can be found by converting X to a random variable Z that is normally distributed with mean 0 and variance 1.

$$Pr(X \geq 13.5) = Pr\left[\frac{X - \mu}{\sigma} \geq \frac{13.5 - \mu}{\sigma}\right]$$

$$= Pr\left[Z \geq \frac{13.5 - 12}{1.8}\right]$$

$$= Pr(Z \geq 0.83)$$

From the table on page 275, this is found to be

$$= 0.2033.$$

Thus, about 20 percent of these miniature poodles have heights that are greater than 14 inches.

z	.00	.01	.02	.03	.04	.05	.06	.07	.08	.09
0.0	.0000	.0040	.0080	.0120	.0160	.0199	.0239	.0279	.0319	.0359
0.1	.0398	.0438	.0478	.0517	.0557	.0596	.0636	.0675	.0714	.0753
0.2	.0793	.0832	.0871	.0910	.0948	.0987	.1026	.1064	.1103	.1141
0.3	.1179	.1217	.1255	.1293	.1331	.1368	.1406	.1443	.1480	.1517
0.4	.1554	.1591	.1628	.1664	.1700	.1736	.1772	.1808	.1844	.1879
0.5	.1915	.1950	.1985	.2019	.2054	.2088	.2123	.2157	.2190	.2224
0.6	.2257	.2291	.2324	.2357	.2389	.2422	.2454	.2486	.2518	.2549
0.7	.2580	2.612	.2642	.2673	.2704	.2734	.2764	.2794	.2823	.2852
0.8	.2881	.2910	.2939	.2967	.2995	.3023	.3051	.3078	.3106	.3133
0.9	.3159	.3186	.3212	.3238	.3264	.3289	.3315	.3340	.3365	.3389
1.0	.3413	.3438	.3461	.3485	.3508	.3531	.3554	.3577	.3599	.3621
1.1	.3643	.3665	.3686	.3708	.3729	.3749	.3770	.3790	.3810	.3830
1.2	.3849	.3869	.3888	.3907	.3925	.3944	.3962	.3980	.3997	.4014
1.3	.4032	.4049	.4066	.4082	.4099	.4115	.4131	.4147	.4162	.4177
1.4	.4192	.4207	.4222	.4236	.4251	.4265	.4279	.4292	.4306	.4319
1.5	.4332	.4345	.4357	.4370	.4382	.4394	.4406	.4418	.4429	.4441
1.6	.4452	.4463	.4474	.4484	.4495	.4505	.4515	.4525	.4535	.4545
1.7	.4554	.4564	.4573	.4582	.4591	.4599	.4608	.4616	.4625	.4633
1.8	.4641	.4649	.4656	.4664	.4671	.4678	.4686	.4693	.4699	.4706
1.9	.4713	.4719	.4726	.4732	.4738	.4744	.4750	4756	.4761	.4767
2.0	.4772	.4778	.4783	.4788	.4793	.4798	.4803	.4808	.4812	.4817
2.1	.4821	.4826	.4830	.4834	.4838	.4842	.4846	.4850	.4854	.4857
2.2	.4861	.4864	.4868	.4871	.4875	.4878	.4881	.4884	.4887	.4890
2.3	.4893	.4896	.4898	.4901	.4904	.4906	.4909	4911	.4913	.4916
2.4	.4918	.4920	.4922	.4925	.4927	.4929	.4931	.4932	.4934	.4936
2.5	.4938	.4940	.4941	.4943	.4945	.4946	.4948	.4949	.4951	.4952
2.6	.4953	.4955	.4956	.4957	.4959	.4960	.4961	.4962	.4963	.4964
2.7	.4965	.4966	.4967	.4968	.4969	.4970	.4971	.4972	.4973	.4974
2.8	.4974	.4975	.4976	.4977	.4977	.4978	.4979	.4979	.4980	.4981
2.9	.4981	.4982	.4983	.4983	.4984	.4984	.4985	.4985	.4986	.4986
3.0	.4987									
3.5	.4997									
4.0	.4999									

Table for the standard normal distribution